Mr. President:

Millions of Progressive-minded, hardworking Americans disagree with your view of what's good for America. We disagree with the massive transfer of national wealth from the working poor to the already rich, which you have made the cornerstone of your policies and programs. We do not applaud your most recent role as Robin Hood-in-reverse. The price for pleasing your millionaire friends, for deploying your trillion-dollar defense buildup, for paving over our national parks and for lining corporate coffers is high . . . . way too high. And we're not going to pay it.

A hollow threat? Not at all, so long as we can overcome a hang-up we've been carrying around in our intellectual baggage for decades. Since the New Deal, the notion that paying one's taxes *automatically* results in a socially desirable transfer of income from the have's to the have-nots, has wound its way deep into our Progressive Ethic. *Face it— it's not true. At least, not now.*

Deduct This Book!*

How Not To Pay Taxes While Ronald Reagan Is President

By J. Peter Segall

Grove Press, Inc./New York

*With apologies to Abbie Hoffman

This book is dedicated
To those who that being out of work
is the surest, cruelest tax-avoidance device of all.

Thank you Lisl and Sydney; Jim, Bob, Rob and Linda; Beth and Sheila; Gloria, Ed, Kay, Zane, Neil, Roget and John and his quotees; those who plug this book, those who buy it, and tons to you, love.

First Evergreen Edition 1983
First Printing 1983
ISBN 0-394-62009-7
Library of Congress Catalog Card Number 83-048404

Manufactured in the United States of America

GROVE PRESS, INC., 196 West Houston Street,
New York, N.Y., 10014

5   4   3   2   1

CONTENTS

"Gimme, gimme shelter—Or I'm gonna fade away . . . ."

Michael Philip Jagger
Master's Candidate, London School of Economics

Introduction

> "*Always kindly, restrained and prepared to forgive an enemy, he (Peisistratus the Tyrant) also lent money to the poorer classes to help them make a living as farmers; and in this his object was twofold. First, it would scatter them over the countryside and prevent a crowd of indigent folk from idling away their time in the Capital; and secondly, by making sure that they were reasonably well off and busy about their private occupations, it would deprive them of the time and even of the wish to meddle in affairs of state. Simultaneously, the tyrant's own revenues were increased, for he levied a tax of one-tenth on all agricultural produce.*"

> Aristotle, circa 325 B.C.
> Describing the Peisistratid Tyranny and offering an early observation of Kemp-Roth economics at work.

Tax Shelter? Who—*me?*

Yes, *you.*

The time has come for you, Tom and Tammy Taxpayer, the unsung John and Jane Doe of our national fiscal fortunes, to think the unthinkable: that *you too*, like hundreds of Americans earning $200,000 and more, don't have to pay taxes.*

You don't have to be rich not to pay taxes. You don't have to be a Fortune 500 conglomerate, hiring high-priced talent trained in the artful dodge, not to pay taxes. You don't have to be a white, Anglo Saxon, middle-aged upper-middle-class white-collar male, in order to wise up to the fact that paying taxes is not the key to heaven, an eternal burden of good citizenship or a badge of honor.

This book has two purposes:

• A strictly *financial* purpose: to show *you*, the average wage-earning American, how to pay less federal income taxes *legally*.

---

* In 1980, according to the Internal Revenue Service, 198 persons earning $200,000-plus, paid no federal income tax. Countless hundreds more paid far less taxes than their earning levels would warrant.

• A strictly *political* purpose: to show you, the Progressive American, how you can stop subsidizing the programs and policies of an Administration you do not support, and how to put those same tax dollars to work instead in support of activities you *do* believe in.

What's A Tax Shelter

Each of the chapters which follow describes legitimate, legal devices which permit *you* to *save* taxes, and *direct* that money elsewhere. Most of these devices might be called "tax shelters," a term as old as Woodrow Wilson's 70-year old-graduated federal income tax itself, but which has acquired a public image as unsavory and un-American as any in our entire political lexicon. To enhance your reading pleasure, Tom and Tammy Taxpayer, and to be able to face yourself each morning in the bathroom mirror—forget whatever evil preconceptions the words "tax shelter" conjure up. Let's pause, just for a second, to look at the term a little bit more closely: what does "tax shelter" mean?

A "tax," says Blacks Law Dictionary, is "a pecuniary burden laid upon individuals or property to support the government." Note well, dear reader: nothing in that definition about equity; i.e., who should pay how much. Note also: taxes *by definition* "support the government," and its agenda, its programs and its priorities—whether *you* do or not.

That leaves us with the word "shelter," which we all know is one of *Homo Sapiens'* three most primal needs. (The PR men of Woodrow Wilson's time must have rejected "tax food" and "tax sex" as too far afield; why they picked "shelter" to dump on is not known.) So you see, it's really quite simple: taxes—like the sun, the rain, the cold and the heat—are one of the basic elements of our existence on this planet responsible for our way of life . . . . but they are also an element which we *must* shelter ourselves against in excess. And just as the well-to-do had caves first, parasols first, and central air conditioning first, so too is it natural that they would be the first to appreciate and appropriate the "tax shelter" to their own as well.

So much for tax shelters in theory . . . . how do they operate in practice? All tax shelters have *one* simple common denominator: they permit you to *avoid* paying taxes by devoting a specific amount of funds to some other purpose instead. The two amounts involved—how much you save in taxes, and how much you devote to this other purpose—need not be the same amount; in fact they rarely are.

Bear in mind that besides this single characteristic common to all tax shelters, they can be as different from each other as pussy cats and Bengal tigers—knowing the species of beast tells you little if anything about the actual animal you're dealing with. In the pages that follow you will read about shelters that require up to thousands of dollars in up-front investments, and others that require little if any up-front cash at all. You will discover shelters that would, if properly taken advantage of, have a profound effect upon your lifestyle—and others that demand barely a minute of your attention.

Three Tax Shelter Categories

Given the literally hundreds of varieties of tax shelters which exist, it is still possible to classify just about all of them into three categories, based on the tax-related *results* they achieve. These result-oriented categories are:

(1) *Outright Permanent Savings.* There are some devices in the tax code which permit direct, permanent tax savings to those who are aware and take advantage of them. Deductions for casualty losses, medical expenses, and charitable contributions fall into this category: the gains one derives from using them are "forever;" that is, they are rarely subject to "recapture" by the taxman in any form.

(2) *Deferral.* By far the lion's share of tax shelters are designed with one overriding purpose in mind: to permit the taxpayer to *postpone* paying Uncle Sam the taxes she owes. As we will see, this is usually accomplished by enabling the

taxpayer to incur paper "losses," which are deductible from
unrelated income before such losses actually occur in fact
(if indeed they *ever* occur!). Don't underestimate the power
of such postponement, or "deferral;" it's no small fortune-
builder if it's used properly. Consider, for instance, that if
prevailing interest rates are 11 percent and you are able, by
grace of deferral, to pay $10,000 in taxes five years later than
originally due, then that $10,000 invested at monthly com-
pounded interest will earn you an additional $7,289.16! (How
this deferral is accomplished—often by a method known as
"accelerated depreciation"—we will discuss later.)

(3) *Conversion.* If a shelter is designed merely to defer
taxes owed, then those taxes will probably have to be paid
sooner or later, and the taxpayer's gain is through the
interest-free use of this money during the interim.

It's a very different story, however, if the tax shelter *also*
permits the taxpayer to *convert* one form of income—the kind
he earns in wages and interest, called "ordinary" income—
into another form, the kind earned through the sale or exchange of appreciated capital assets—called "capital gains"
income. This is so because the tax laws treat these two kinds
of income very differently, favoring the latter by allowing
a "capital gains" deduction in the amount of 60 percent of
net capital gain.

To illustrate: Suppose that you, Tom and Tammy Taxpayer, have combined taxable 1982 income of $30,000. Your
1982 marginal tax rate—the rate of tax you would pay on
an *additional* dollar of income—is 33 percent. Now suppose
your wage income is increased by $500. This is treated as
ordinary income; hence, it is subject to a 33 percent tax, leaving you with $335. Now suppose instead that you have made
a $500 profit through the sale of 100 shares of stock in Eco
Energy Systems, Inc., and that you owned the stock more
than 12 months, thereby qualifying the profits upon sale as
long-term capital gains. Fully 60 percent of that gain is sub-
tracted first [$500 − (60% × 500) = $200] which is then
multiplied by your 33 percent marginal rate to leave you

owing only $66 in taxes, for a net after-tax gain of $434. So
you can see that when you can use some legitimate tax-
shelter hocus-pocus to convert ordinary income into capital
gains income, there are actual tax-savings in store for you.

Conversion, then, is the other major feature which, along
with deferral, gives tax shelters their reason-for-being. And
when one finds a shelter which couples these two features
with outright, permanent savings, without any significant
long-run drawbacks—well then, it's time to *move*.

What This Book Is For

This book is not designed to be and should not be used
as a compendium of every conceivable tax-saving device the
Internal Revenue Code has to offer. You should know, for
instance, that you can drill for oil and natural gas, breed
racehorses, raise cattle, print lithographs, underwrite a major motion picture, sail a yacht and fly your own jet plane,
all at substantially less cost to you personally than would
be the case had not some enterprising congressmen and
enlightened entrepreneurs invented tax shelters for these
sorts of activities. Any certified public accountant or tax attorney can provide you with a pre-packaged investment pro-
posal (commonly called a "prospectus") which would permit
you to participate along with thousands of other faceless investors in partnerships (commonly called "syndications") to
drill for oil, breed racehorses, etc.

The tax code also contains numerous other income-
offsetting devices which you should know and take advantage of: deductions for catastrophic losses, certain medical
expenses, state and local taxes paid, income-averaging and
so on. You should know that all these various sorts of shelters
and tax-saving devices exist. But you should also be aware
that some shelters serve to further what might be called
"socially desirable purposes," more than others. You can *also*
rehabilitate and restore a decaying building, insulate or
solarize a home, support a candidate for public office, operate
a day care center, conserve farmland, save for your kid's col-

lege education, and save taxes too. All these activities can
be tax-favored pursuits too; yet many of them seem to be
the best-kept secrets of the world of tax shelters despite their
importance to society as a whole.

These "white sheep" of the tax shelter world are the
honored subject of this book. But before we look at them
individually and apply each of them to your own financial
circumstances, Tom and Tammy Taxpayer, there are five
basic general principles about taxpaying and taxsaving to
learn.

These principles are very simple—but very important:

1. *An extra dollar in taxes saved is worth alot more than
   an extra dollar in income earned.*

2. *Tax avoidance, unlike tax evasion, is a wholly
   honorable pursuit.*

3. *Taxsaving is a year-round way of life—not an April
   15th afterthought.*

4. *Taxpaying is not a politically neutral act. (Or: "I am
   mad as hell. And I'm not going to subsidize it anymore.")*

5. *Tax shelters turn Uncle Sam into your very own rich
   uncle.*

Let's briefly examine each of these principles in turn.

1. An extra dollar in taxes saved is worth alot more than an extra dollar in income earned.

Had Confucius been an accountant, this proposition
could have become a fortune-cookie favorite, for the seeds
of fortunes are surely here.

Suppose again, Tom and Tammy Taxpayer, that your
taxable income this year will amount to $30,000. This would

put you in the 33 percent "marginal tax bracket," meaning the following: that were you to earn one extra dollar of income, you would be able to keep 67 cents of that dollar as after-tax income, and 33 cents would go to the Treasury in federal taxes.

Now suppose, instead, that through the magic of *any* form of legal tax avoidance, the *amount of taxes* you owe is reduced by one dollar (NOT your taxable income—the actual taxes you owe). That dollar in taxes saved amounts to a dollar of extra income to you—but *none* of *it* is taxable! In other words: that dollar in extra income you earned gets you only 67 cents in disposable after-tax income, but that extra dollar you saved in taxes owed gets you a full dollar— it's worth 50 percent more!

It's easy to see that this discrepancy in value between extra-dollars earned and extra-dollars-in-taxes-saved, increases the more the taxpayer earns, and the higher his or her marginal tax rate.*

* Here are examples of marginal tax rates for taxpayers of different incomes. Because our tax system is "progressive," you will note that the tax rate increases with income levels:

Taxable Income		Marginal Tax Rate If You Are:	
	Single	Married	Head of Household
$10,000			
Tax Year 1982	19%	16%	20%
1983	17	15	18
1984	16	14	17
$20,000			
1982	31	22	28
1983	28	19	25
1984	26	18	24
$30,000			
1982	40	33	38
1983	36	30	34
1984	34	28	32
$40,000			
1982	49	39	43
1983	44	35	44
1984	40	33	40
$100,000			
1982	50	50	50
1983	50	50	50
1984	50	45	50

For a single taxpayer earning $50,000 a year, at a correspond-
ing 1982 marginal rate of 50 percent, an extra tax dollar
saved is actually worth twice as much as the extra dollar
earned.

This should explain why high-earners have traditionally
been more interested in tax-sheltering devices than low-
earners. But it also points up a curious phenomenon regarding the way *all of us* deal with our need to come by more
spending money as inflation forces the cost of essential goods
ever higher. We try to *earn* more. According to the Bureau
of Labor Statistics, in more than 52 percent of all American
households both spouses are income-earners today, up sharply from a decade ago. The number of "moonlighters"—
primary wage-earners taking on a second job—has increased
half a million since 1973. One has to wonder, keeping this
dollars-earned versus tax dollars-saved principle in mind,
whether some of these second-earners and moonlighters
wouldn't be better off putting the same amount of time and
energy into legal, effective tax avoidance!

2. **Tax avoidance, unlike tax evasion, is a wholly honorable
    pursuit.**

Those who practice tax avoidance include some of the
most highly paid attorneys and accountants in the country.
Those who practice tax evasion may average a couple of
bucks an hour stamping out license plates in prisons around
the nation. Obviously, there are important differences between these two concepts worth mastering.

Simply stated, tax *avoidance* is the act of not paying
taxes otherwise owed through the use of any *legal* device;
tax *evasion* is the non-payment of taxes through *illegal*
means. Fair enough. Sometimes there is just no mistaking
which is which. For instance, the restaurant waiter who
"overlooks" declaring $20,000 in tip-income along with his
$6,500 in wages is clearly evading his tax obligation, and
could be subject to civil and criminal sanctions for doing so.

But sometimes the distinctions seem to blur. Consider, for example, the celebrated case of the married couple who, for several years running, divorced shortly before New Years and re-married a couple of days after. Their logic for doing so was open and notorious: the federal tax laws impose a "penalty" upon married taxpayers (see Chapter 12), a penalty which this couple was willing to "avoid" by altering their marital status at predictable intervals. The Internal Revenue Service was not taken, to say the least, with the prospect of a widespread well-timed marital discord-reconciliation cycle wreaking havoc on the national balance sheet. In 1976 it issued a revenue ruling—the device through which it often deals with such questions—concluding that such divorces were "shams" and would not be "honored" for tax purposes.

This example is not an isolated one, and it highlights the general rule regarding tax shelters of all kinds: any undertaking which cannot be justified by any reasonable expectation of gain or legitimate purpose other than the tax ramifications alone, is likely to be frowned upon—and an attempt made to disallow it—by the Internal Revenue Service.

3. Taxsaving is a year-round way of life—not an April 15th afterthought.

If you have a wife and 2.2 kids and stationwagon to support, as the average of us do, it is improbable that you would wait until the day your bi-weekly paycheck is due, and then start figuring out how to earn the next one. And if you are compensated for your labors the way most Americans are, then you are probably accustomed to doing your work over a specific period, say, two weeks, and getting paid for it afterward—in other words, you've trained yourself to perform your tasks on an ongoing, regular basis, knowing you will be remunerated for your time and effort on an ongoing, regular basis. Gainful employment is a state of mind; it involves planning and forethought, patience and anticipation, restraint and reward. So, as a matter of fact, does paying taxes—and *not* paying taxes. Good household budgeting calls for you to sit down, maybe once a month or so, and pay the bills; let's assume that's what you do. Yet your *biggest* household bill, year in and year out, is almost certainly your federal income tax bill—how much regular, monthly attention do you give *it*?

Up comes the most logical question: how can I think about taxes once a month, when I find out what I owe only at the end of the year? It may be a logical question but it's not really an honest one—because, if you think about it, the federal income tax withholding your employer does for you every pay period is—if it's being done accurately—an on-the-ball *prediction* of the taxes *you* will owe come April 15 (see Chapter 1). That little bit of information is *absolutely critical* when it comes to sheltering your income from taxes; it tells you, first of all, what marginal tax bracket you can expect to fall in this year. It tells you, second, how much taxes you will likely owe—and conversely, how much you can *save*. (You *must* understand that just because taxes have been withheld from your pay, it *in no way* follows that those taxes are *paid* and lost to you forever. Think of withholding as a means of enforced saving for your benefit; if you come up with enough shelter at the end of the year, potentially every dollar of enforced withholding will come back to you as a refund.)

Effective taxsaving, in short, is a process that begins January 1 of each year and affects your tax status at the *end* of that year. You simply cannot hope to reduce what you owe Uncle Sam to any degree if you begin to *think* about it around tax time; with rare exceptions, it's a hopeless cause by then.*

So, Tom and Tammy Taxpayer, here's the bad news: *saving taxes is a year-round way of life, not an April 15th afterthought.* It should receive as much attention as you give your

* One tax lawyer I know likes to joke about the way most bookstores put all their tax guides on the shelf around early December—apparently they make great Christmas gifts—and then take them off just after April 15th. The store-owners are just responding to supply and demand—and people just don't want to "plan" on saving taxes until it's too damn late!

sources of income (it *is* a source of income!) and your monthly bills (it *is* your *biggest* bill!). But you've already heard the good news: a dollar in taxes saved is worth a whole lot more than a dollar in income earned.

Here's a challenge to you. This weekend, gather your 1982 withholding information together (and your spouse's, if he or she works too). Figure out the taxes you're likely to owe at the end of *1983*. Write the figure down at the top of the first page of a big fat legal pad. On a separate piece of paper, start keeping track of the number of hours you and your spouse will put into taxplanning this year. At the end of the year, calculate the number of tax dollars you've saved through all the methods you ultimately use and divide it by the total number of hours you've put in; then compare that hourly rate with the rate you both get paid on the job. If the taxplanning figure isn't *at least double* what you make at work . . . . well, I'll be very surprised (I said this was a challenge, not a money-back guarantee).

4. Taxpaying is not a politically neutral act. (Or: "I am mad as hell. And I'm not going to subsidize it anymore.")

Hark back to the definition of "tax"—"a pecuniary burden laid upon individuals or property *to support the government*." In 1981, individual income taxes accounted for an estimated $252 billion in federal revenues, or 45 percent of all monies taken in by the federal government. Our Gross National Product that year was an estimated $2.9 trillion; in other words, almost 10 percent of our total GNP found its way to the Treasury in the form of individual income tax collections.

Recently there was much talk throughout the land of the importance to our national economic health of an across-the-board income tax cut. Ronald Reagan campaigned on, and won the White House largely on the basis of, his commitment to an economic program he promised would "help create

13 million new jobs;"* have an immediate impact on the economic viability of the nation,** and bring federal deficit spending under control.***

Since then, and since the tax cut Mr. Reagan spoke of was enacted into law, we've had record 11 percent unemployment and much talk of annual national deficits in the $200 billion-plus range, to contend with. To lower those deficits drastically the President, with Congressional approval, has taken a blow-torch to numerous so-called "social programs."

Who's been helped and hurt most by this peculiar combination of drastic tax cuts, drastic social spending cuts and surged defense spending—an estimated $1.6 trillion more over the next five years—that is Reaganomics? The kindest word one can offer is that the jury is still out on that question. A more honest answer is that study after study is showing Reaganomics fueling the shift of a steadily greater share of the national income, into the hands of the rich.

One study, for the Washington-based Urban Institute, finds that the Reagan-inspired 1981 Economic Recovery Tax Act will, by 1984, increase the share of after-tax income for those whose after-tax incomes are $50,000 and higher, while decreasing the share for those whose after-tax incomes are $10,000 or less. (That's taking the effects of the tax act *alone*, not counting the effect of massive spending cuts on the poor.)****

Another study forcasts the combined effect of the Reagan tax and spending cuts will be to deprive American families in the bottom one-fifth of the income scale of $1.2 billion in cash income, while those in the top one-fifth would gain $36 billion.

---

* February 18, 1981 Presidential message to Congress.
** March 10, 1981 Presidential message to Congress.
*** July 27, 1981 Presidential message to Congress. All three of the above are cited in Palmer, John L., and Sawhill, Isabel V., Eds; *The Reagan Experiment*. Washington, D.C., The Urban Institute Press, 1982.
***** Hulten, Charles R., and O'Neill, June A., "Tax Policy," in *The Reagan Experiment*. Washington, D.C., The Urban Institute Press, 1982, P. 120.

Still a third effort, by the Congressional Budget Office, sees that a household with less than $10,000 in income will, by 1985, be out $140 by virtue of the Reagan economic program, while a household earning over $80,000 would be ahead $21,860.

No clearthinking American can deny that the Reagan Administration has achieved a wholesale re-orientation of federal spending priorities by its careful jiggling of tax rates, tax preferences and expenditures. Hundreds of thousands of working-class citizens have demonstrated in Washington. Organized labor, minorities and other representatives of the working and non-working poor are vowing loud opposition in Congressional and Presidential elections to come.

But just about all of us, confound it, keep on paying our taxes like the good little law-abiding H & R Blockheads we are.

Just about all of us. There are a growing number of "tax rebels," to use columnist Mary McGrory's apt phrase, and at the head of the pack is Raymond Hunthausen of Seattle. On April 15, 1982, Hunthausen sent the U.S. Treasury a check for $125, precisely one-half the amount of federal income tax due on his $9,000 salary. An avowed opponent of the nuclear arms race, Hunthausen placed the other $125 in an escrow account for something called the "World Peace Fund," an entity not yet in existence but which, if legislation promoting it becomes law, will permit other tax rebels like Hunthausen to give the fund the "military portion" of the federal income taxes they owe.

Asked at a press conference whether he was willing to go to jail for his self-proclaimed act of tax *evasion* (unfortunately the good teachings of this book were not available at the time), he proclaimed that he surely was. "I think the teachings of Jesus tell us to render to a nuclear-arms Caesar what Caesar deserves: tax resistance," Hunthausen told his congregation.

That's right—congregation. Mr. Hunthausen, tax rebel with a holy cause, is the Roman Catholic Archbishop of

Seattle. And Hunthausen is far from alone. According to IRS
Commissioner Roscoe Egger, some 20,000 "tax protestors"
using or promoting illegal tax-evading methods have been
identified, and his agency has adopted a "stern, no nonsense
approach," including seeking jail sentences in some instances, to stop them in their tracks. "They are clearly a
threat to our system of voluntary compliance," he says.*

So, of course, were those young men who refused under
threat of imprisonment to be drafted into fighting a war they
couldn't support. So were those women who took on the law
in order to win the right to vote; those blacks who risked
life and limb to end slavery; those workers branded com-
munists who won the right to form unions. All of them fought
politically noble wars with whatever appropriate political
tools were at their disposal at the time. But what's different
this time, and what makes the tax rebel a comfortably off
creature in comparison with his predecessors, is that his
arsenal *can* consist of tax-avoiding devices that are *lawful*
in every respect.

Start thinking of your 1040 Form as your ballot. It gives
you a heckuva lot more options than your 1980 Presidential
ballot did, and you shouldn't be shy about using them.

5. Tax shelters turn Uncle Sam into your very own rich uncle.

Let's say you decide to invest in a real-estate limited-
partnership tax shelter. More about the intricate details of
limited partnerships later; for now, understand that such an
investment is a classic "deferral"-type tax shelter, in that
it gives the participant the chance to postpone, through
"depreciation," paying taxes for a long period of years. When
the property is ultimately sold, however, a certain amount
of that depreciation has to be paid; it is "recaptured." You,
of course, are the one who gets to pick the real estate to invest in, not Ronald Reagan. Yet realize that it's *his* money
you're investing during the course of the tax shelter. If it

* Remarks by Commissioner Egger before the Heart of America Tax Institute, October 6, 1981. More on this subject in Chapter 14.

does well, and the price goes up, the sale will net you greater profits, a portion of which you will have to give over to the President in capital gains tax—you both win. If it does poorly, and the price of the property goes down, there will be less depreciation-recapture and less taxes ultimately owed—you both lose.

Do you see what's happening! Never again should you fret that you were born without a rich uncle, a sugardaddy to sew the seed capital from whence your own personal fortune shall bloom. You *do* have one! He lives in Washington, D.C.—he *is* Washington, D.C.! Better still, he will never die . . . . he will never criticize your investment judgment (although his "accountant," the Commissioner of Internal Revenue, may call you in for a talk if he thinks you're getting greedy). His pocket is virtually bottomless, limited only by your own creativity, and you have no competing nephews or nieces to worry about. And if you do make a bad misjudgment, he will always be there to help bail you out and set you up to try again. Uncle Sam's personal policies may be distasteful to you, but no matter . . . . you can get him to help solarize your home, support the most liberal of political candidates, underwrite your child's college education . . . . you name it! He's really quite a guy, and it's past time you made him a silent partner in your financial future.

So much for the five principles. There's work to be done.

1

Overwithholding—The Interest-Free Loan For Billions Uncle Sam Gets From You

Overwithholding is, without serious question, simply the biggest single mistake a taxpayer—especially a Progressive taxpayer—can make. The law says that your employer must withhold 80 percent of what the properly applied formulas predict you will owe the IRS in taxes on your wage income at the end of the year, and no more. Yet come April 15 of every year, most taxpayers complete their 1040's to discover to their jubilation that they are due a sizable refund—totally oblivious to the fact that they have given the government—specifically, the Reagan Administration—an interest-free loan for *billions*.

Come on, you say. You must be exaggerating. *Not a bit.* To use the IRS' own estimates: For tax year 1981, a total of just under 95.5 million income tax returns were filed. And of that number, almost 72 million were eligible for refunds due to overwithholding. That's almost 75 percent of all returns, or three out of every four returns filed. And the total amount of their overpayments came to *$55,100,000,000.* We are talking about over *fifty billion dollars.* Not too suprisingly, overwithholders tend to be younger, salaried rather than self-employed, and in the lower income range. And guess what? Of the 72 million taxpayers who overpaid, around 17 million filed what the IRS calls "nontaxable returns"—that is, returns filed by taxpayers who for varying reasons actually owed *no* income tax, and were therefore entitled to a refund of *every dime* withheld from their paychecks.*

Why is it so? It would be a simple "out" to blame it all on the system, on withholding formulas that seem calculatedly complex, on conspiratorial bureaucratic forces that act like loan sharks snapping at your heels with hidden costs, and

---

* *1982 Annual Report,* Commission and Chief Counsel, Internal Revenue Service, Washington, D.C., 1983, P.7. 1982.

so on. But the real blame has to lie once again with *us*—
with the amazing lack of attention *we* give the annual taxpaying ritual, and how we run for our blinders whenever the
taxman cometh out-of-season.

How Overwithholding Affects You

We'll explore the details in a minute, but first let's take
a look at how overwithholding affects *you*. Suppose you
receive your paycheck bi-weekly (26 times a year), and that
each paycheck overwithholds your income by five percent.
If you earn $25,000 annually, this overwithholding amounts
to $1,250 a year, or $48 each paycheck. Now suppose that
midway through the year you buy a house, a first-time home
purchase. The tax-deductible portion of your settlement costs
(see Chapter 4) come to $1,000 and your monthly mortgage
payments are $800, $750 of which represents payment of
mortgage interest. Assuming you're in the 32 percent
marginal tax rate bracket you will be entitled thereby to additional tax savings in the neighborhood of:

$$(.32 \times \$1,000) + (.32 \times \$750 \times 6 \text{ months}) = \$1,760$$

for the rest of the year. If you work for the entire year without
adjusting your withholding allowances from where they were
on January 1, your aggregate overwithholding will now
amount to $3,010.

Now, forget what you just read. Imagine, instead, that
you turn on the TV one night, and there is the President of
the United States, speaking from the Oval Office about the
sad state of the nation's fiscal affairs. He offers a breath-
taking new plan to save the country, which consists of bor-
rowing $3,010 from every able-bodied average wage-earning
American, interest-free for one year, to help pay off the national debt. He's made the plan into an Executive Order
which goes into effect tomorrow, and advises you to have
the funds ready to hand over, in 26 equal installments, beginning next payday.

Of course it's ludicrous. You wouldn't stand for it, in principle and because you simply can't afford to fork Washington

over an interest-free loan for *any* amount on top of the taxes
you now pay. But that is *exactly* what you *are* doing if you,
like about 71 million of your fellow citizens, fail to take the
five minutes it takes to calculate your withholding properly
and make the necessary adjustments. Worse yet, you may
count yourself among the four out of every ten salaried taxpayers who, according to a 1980 survey, deliberately "ensure their refund" by claiming fewer allowances than they
know they're entitled to.

The traditional view held by so many taxpaying wage-
earners is that we don't want to get stuck with an unexpected
tax bill at the end of the year. We treat the chance to enter
a positive refund amount on our tax return as if it were a
delightsome gift from above. Never forget it—those are *your*
hard-earned dollars Uncle Sam is giving you back, dollars
that he's had to hold and spend his way, interest-free, since
the day you earned them. Of course, the reverse also holds
true—any amount you owe at year's end technically amounts
to an interest-free loan of taxes from Uncle Sam to you.*
That's why your goal ought to be not to withhold one red
cent more than you are legally obliged to withhold.

Withholding Rates Versus Tax Rates

One reason overwithholding occurs so often is that many
of us confuse "withholding rates" with actual "tax rates."
In fact, tax rates are the formulas used to calculate what
amount of taxes you actually owe; withholding rates, on the
other hand, are indices used by your payroll clerk at the
government's behest to make a best-guess estimate of what
taxes you are likely to owe. So if you only work half a year,
or get married during the year, or if you have a second wage-
earner in the family, or if you buy a home at mid-year—your
year-end tax-rates will *automatically* reflect these
developments (provided you take the proper tax deductions),
but your withholding rates *won't*.

Withholding rates are generally expressed as a statement
of your family life. For example, a married wage-earner with

---

* Based on the theory that you owe taxes on income as of the day you
receive it, not as of the end of the year.

a spouse and two children perhaps would choose to elect an "MO4" rate (otherwise known as married with four exemptions—one each for himself, wife and each child). This is where the misconception begins. Instead of the Internal Revenue Service establishing a simple percentage rate method for the taxpayer to follow, the taxpayer gets the feeling that he should not claim more exemptions than he has dependents. This is a major root-cause of overwithholding!

Calculating The Right Withholding Rate

On the reverse of the W-4 form (the form you complete when you begin work with a new employer), there is a worksheet to assist you in calculating the proper number of exemptions. This worksheet takes into account the number of dependents you have, as well as the amount of deductions you anticipate in the coming year; any other adjustments to gross income may also be included. You are basically given the opportunity to prepare an early, hypothetical tax return, based on the knowledge you have at the time you prepare the form. Then, you establish your withholding rate based on the methods contained on the form. Should your situation change (i.e., your spouse's salary changes, you gain additional deductions, or a new dependent), remember to update this withholding form with your employer.

An easy tax-planning device is to use the previous year's tax return as a basis for figuring this year's withholding rates. If you received a refund in excess of $500 on last year's taxes, you definitely need to take a good look at your withholding rates.

If you received a large refund last year here is an easy way to increase your net spendable income. Let's say you got a $1,000 refund last year. Take a "safe" percentage of the refund—say, 60 percent, or $600—and divide it by the number of paydays you get in a year. For example, if you are paid weekly, divide by 52; if your are paid bi-weekly, divide by 26; semi-monthly, divide by 24, etc. In our example let's say we are paid bi-weekly. We then divide 600 by 26 to get an average $23 per payday that we could safely

increase our net pay (assuming there have been no significant changes since last year). Now go see your company
payroll clerk and tell him you want to adjust your
withholding so that you get an additional $23 in each
paycheck. It's that simple.

Withholding Only Of Wages

Also, don't overlook the possibility that your employer
may not be withholding your income properly. First of all,
withholding only applies to *wages*—defined as "all remuneration (other than fees paid to a public official) for services performed by an employee for his employer, including the cash
value of all remuneration paid in any medium other than
cash." Accordingly, non-wage payments from your
employer—for instance, an advance or reimbursement of
business travelling expenses or employee moving costs—
are not subject to withholding. Neither are, among other
items, the value of nominal gifts given on a holiday like
Christmas; pensions or annuities paid over more than one
year; contributions to your tax-exempt Individual Retirement Account (IRA); group term life insurance payments for
policy coverage up to $50,000, or educational-assistance plan
payments (if they would not be includable as income), work-
man's compensation benefits and reimbursements for
medical care or permanent injury payments. As to so-called
"supplemental wages"—bonuses, commissions, overtime
pay—an employer in most cases may choose at her discre-
tion to treat these as separate from your regular wages and
impose a flat, 20 percent withholding rate, and it may be
worth your while to encourage your employer to make this
election. If you expect to be eligible for the earned income
credit due to your overall low-income level, you can request
an advance on this credit to be applied against your
withholding. And, perhaps most importantly, if you
reasonably anticipate a large number of itemized deductions,
you may claim extra withholding exemptions, using the

worksheet provided on page 2 of your W-4 withholding form. If you are one member of a two-earner married couple, don't forget to take into account a special deduction for people in your situation (which for 1983 will equal ten percent of the lesser of $30,000 or of the qualified earned income of the spouse with the lower income).

Employee Versus Contractor

Second, withholding only applies to "employees," as distinguished from "independent contractors." The distinction is one upon which lawyers have heaped many billable hours; essentially it turns upon whether the person for whom the services are rendered has *the right* to direct or control the means and methods used to achieve the objective. If that right to direct and control is present, then the service-provider is an employee (whether or not the employer actually exercises the right); if it is not present, then the provider is an independent contractor, not subject to withholding by the employer (but subject to "estimated tax" payments applicable to the self-employed).

A couple of other final points. If you had no income tax liability for the preceding year, and can certify to your employer that you anticipate none for the current year as well, then you can be exempt from withholding. This total exemption, designed primarily for student part-time workers or those with very large deductions, can be claimed by using line 6 of your W-4 form.

Please—please—don't think you can avoid the perils of withholding by not filing a W-4 form. If you are a wage-earning employee, there is no such thing as "withholding evasion;" withholding will *automatically* occur from your paycheck, but at a rate applicable as if you were single (i.e., no exemption-eligible dependents) with no other allowances. So you can only do *better* by filing your W-4.

When you do file your W-4, keep a copy handy. And when any major "financial event" occurs in your life, be it the birth of a baby, buying a home, you name it—make sure your W-4 form reflects your new economic reality.

2

Tax-Sheltered Retirement Savings Plans— What They Won't Tell You At The Bank

I.R.A's ... Keoghs ... Tax Deferred Annuities ... the Pentagon talks straighter about top-secret weaponry that can blow up the world; you'd think our financial wizards could communicate more kindly with regard to our (sigh) retirement. Are they trying to HIDE something?

Well ... maybe.

Retirement planning is a science and an art. There is no sensible way to help an individual with his or her retirement-related financial needs without knowing gads about his or her personal financial situation and expectations for later life. So we won't try. But we will take a brief look at one major mechanism that allows you to salt away for those Golden Pond years with sympathetic, 207-year old Uncle Sam right at your side. Retirement tax shelters are today's financial rage, and there's good reason why.

Take the "IRA," or "Individual Retirement Account." An IRA is a way for wage-earning employees, like you, Tom and Tammy Taxpayer, to save some of those earnings for your future retirement needs. (So-called "Keogh Plans" are designed to achieve much the same result for the self-employed, and won't be discussed separately.)

Two Big Tax Advantages

At its simplest level, the IRA offers you two big tax advantages:

One: If you're single, you can put up to $2,000 or 100 percent of your earned income, whichever is less, into an IRA every year until you reach age 70½. If you're married and both of you work, your joint annual contribution ceiling is $4,000; if your spouse doesn't work, it's $2,250. And every cent of your contribution is tax deductible from your federal income tax. The following chart is a simple way of calculating what that tax savings alone would be worth to you, depending on your tax bracket:

| If your tax bracket is: | And you contribute | |
| | $2,000 | $4,000 |
	You will save in taxes:	
20 percent	$400	$800
30 percent	$600	$1,200
40 percent	$800	$1,600
50 percent (top bracket after 1981)	$1,000	$2,000

This deductibility is not forever. This is a classic "deferral"-type tax shelter: you *will* be taxed on your contributions, but only when you ultimately withdraw them from the IRA. And *presumably* you'll be retired by then, in a much lower income bracket.

Two: Whatever *interest* you earn on the funds in your IRA will not be taxed until you start taking the funds out, and then only as you take them out. This deferral feature allows the interest in your IRA to accumulate through compounding at a rate far higher than it would, were you taxed on the accumulation in the year it's earned. This is a phenomenal earning power we're talking about; look how $2,000 invested yearly in an IRA yielding 12 percent per year will grow in 30 years, contrasted with equal-yielding $2,000-per-year *taxed* investments made by individuals in varying tax brackets:

	25% Tax Bracket	40% Tax Bracket	50% Tax Bracket	IRA
Amount Available to Invest	$2,000	$2,000	$2,000	$2,000
Tax	$500	$800	$1,000	-0-
Amount Available After Taxes	$1,500	$1,200	$1,000	2,000
Earnings Rate After Tax	9%	7.2%	6%	12%
Amount at the End of 30 Years	$222,863	$125,976	$83,802	$504,585

(Source: *IRA '82*, E.F. Hutton and Company, Inc., 1982, P. 4.)

Clearly, the 40 percent bracket individual does more than *four* times better with his IRA investment than he would with an equivalent but taxable one. The 50 percent bracket investor does *six-and-a-half* times better!

Convinced? Wait just a second. Recall we said that the money *will* be taxed, after all, when you take it out. And except in the event of death or disability—in which case the funds can be immediately withdrawn—the law creating IRA's intends that withdrawals *may* begin only after you reach the age of 59½, and *must* begin in the tax year you reach 70½.

Must You Wait?

Note, we said that's what the law *intends*. IRA's were not created as a way of sneaking around having to pay taxes for just a couple of years. If you withdraw any funds from your IRA prior to reaching age 59½, those funds will be included as ordinary income in that year—*and in addition*, you will have to pay a *premature withdrawal* penalty equaling 10 percent of the amount you withdraw prematurely.

Whoo boy! A penalty tax! Ten Percent!!! You're shivering. On top of having to pay my regular tax! Never, you say, *never*. Tammy vows to become a bag lady before she'll let you touch your IRA under age 59½. You start making plans to celebrate your fifty-nine-and-one-halfth birthday with a parade down Wall Street.

Hey fella. We'll say it again, and don't you ever forget. Taxpaying is a *political act*. The power *not* to pay taxes is a *political weapon*. The power *not* to pay taxes *now*, and to pay them instead at *some future time*, affects both the people in power now and those in power the day you pay. If *you* can decide *precisely* when that future date will come, you can decide which public officials to help. And if 25 million Progressive-minded Tom and Tammys make the same decision, with several thousand dollars of taxes at stake in each case . . . draw your own conclusions.

IRA's present an unsurpassed opportunity to wield the tax system like a fiscal neutron bomb. Together, we can level David Stockman and leave everything else standing.

So you put $2,000 in an IRA, which earns 12 percent annually, let's say, and you're in the 40 percent tax bracket. Let's assume for the moment that it's a one-time only deposit. Here's what happens over the next five years:

Year	Deposits	Taxes Saved	Interest Earned
1981	$2,000	$800	-0-
1982	-0-	.4 × $240 = $96	$240
1983	-0-	.4 × $268 = $107	$268
1984	-0-	.4 × $301 = $120	$301
1985	-0-	.4 × $337 = $135	$337
Totals	$2,000	$458 on interest $800 on principal	$1,146

By the end of 1985, you will have earned $1,146 in interest on your original $2,000 IRA investment. And because it was tax-sheltered, you will have *deferred* $1,258 in taxes ($458 in tax on interest earned; $800 in tax on your original deposit).

Using Your IRA To Make A Political Statement

Now comes a truly big step in your life: it's time to use the tax system to make an important political statement. And as we go on, *please* keep in mind that it is *not illegal* to withdraw funds from your IRA before you turn 59½ ... just expensive.

In November 1984, a Presidential election will occur. By December of 1985, whoever wins that election will have had nearly 12 months to prove herself, and the worthiness of her program, to you. And then, you will have a chance to decide whether you want to support her program by being taxed *a little more heavily* than you might otherwise be.

Let's presume the new President is better than what's presently in the Oval Office, and you want to support her program. You're still in the same 40 percent tax bracket you were in five years earlier. So . . . wham!!! You take the plunge. You *premature withdraw* your original $2,000 IRA deposit.

In a blinding flash the taxman is at your door, barking as only he can. You owe me $800 plus a $200 penalty, he salivates. Visions of a maximum-security cell in Leavenworth dance before your tear-hazed eyes.

Pay him the $1,000. Give him a cup of coffee. Hug him and kiss him, for he is your best dumb friend. Send him on his raving way and look at what's *really* happened:

You would have had to pay the $800 in taxes on your original deposit anyway, had you not opened the IRA in the first place. Over the last five years that money worked hard for you, earning $1,146 in interest—$458 of which was taxes saved. That $1,146 *still sits* in your IRA. But because you were a little "premature" at wanting your principal back, you paid a little extra for it: 200 bucks extra. Your are *still up $258* in tax savings! And at a "cost" of that 200 bucks, if you want to call it that, you have taken the opportunity of withholding more than $1,200 from the budget of a government you just couldn't support.

Now if that's just too political a rationale for you, look at it this way: let's assume that in 1985 you're 40, and you need to borrow $2,000 until you turn 59½. The interest you would end up paying on that money over 19½ years would be far, far in excess of the $1,000 you forked over to Uncle Sam in order to have your money now.

Now consider this:

• Under the Reagan tax program, individual income tax rates are scheduled to come down substantially over the next two years. So if the amount you earn remains constant, you will be paying proportionately less taxes in the future. The ability to defer paying tax on that $2,000 until 1985, therefore, will give you tax savings that could easily overshadow that measly 10 percent penalty you gotta pay.

Or this:

• Perhaps you can foresee a year in the near future when your income will be drastically reduced—because you'll be going back to school, taking a year off to travel or writing a book on taxes, etc. If that's the case, and you withdraw your IRA principal in that year, you'll pay taxes on it according to your income bracket in that year. You could save a *bundle*. The ten percent tax penalty could dwindle into sheer nothingness in comparison. One word of warning: make sure the financial institution you open your IRA with doesn't impose any major premature withdrawal penalties of its own.

In sum, give some serious thought to the possibility that the Congressionally enacted penalty for early withdrawal from an IRA is, to be polite, a red herring to terrify you into stupified submission and nothing more. Use your IRA investment prudently, but creatively, and teach your friends to do the same. And if you make an early withdrawal for reasons which are at least partly political, make sure you communicate that fact to the elected representatives of your choice.

Where You Can Put Your IRA Funds

There is one other aspect of IRA's worth touching on. And it is that the range of investments you can put your IRA funds in is extremely broad. Banks, savings- and-loan institutions and credit unions, stockbrokers and insurance companies, have all scrambled for a piece of the action. Consequently, you can buy into a money market fund or some other form of interest-bearing instrument; you can buy shares of publicly traded stock; in some instances you can even purchase real estate investments. You can have a banker or broker manage your IRA account just as you would have them advise you on how to invest your after-tax savings, the big difference being that these funds are before-tax, and whatever they earn is tax-sheltered. (Accordingly, it wouldn't make much sense to buy tax-exempt municipal bonds which are already tax-sheltered with your IRA funds.) Alternatively you can create what is known as a "self-directed" IRA, and become your own IRA manager. For details on how to accomplish this, talk to your attorney, accountant, broker or banker. The point is that you can use your IRA to invest in virtually any socially desirable activity you wish—and by using an IRA, Uncle Sam will be investing with you as a silent partner all along the way. Make sure you write him every year and tell him how your joint investments are coming along.

Tax-Sheltered Annuities

If you're a teacher, nurse, or otherwise employed by a non-profit organization, then you ought to be aware of another tax-advantaged savings method that could be right for you. It's called a *Tax-Sheltered Annuity* (TSA), and it works like this: your non-profit employer deducts a set portion of your salary each year and invests it in an "annuity," which is essentially a contractual agreement to pay you (the "annuitant") a specified amount during an agreed-upon set of payment periods later in return for your contributions now. The money the employer sets aside in this manner is tax-deferred, just as in the case of the IRA, and so is any tax on the interest that money earns. As an employee, you can usually contribute a portion of your salary too and it, too, is also exempt from tax until the year you withdraw it. The maximum age for withdrawal from a TSA is 80, not 70 as for IRA's. But even more important, there is no extra tax penalty for premature withdrawal—only the tax you would otherwise owe, based on the tax bracket you're in at the time you make the withdrawal. And in the event you change jobs, or just want to change investments, you can withdraw any or all of your TSA savings and "roll over" the funds into another tax-sheltered retirement savings plan, like an IRA, without having to pay any tax at that time.

Non-profit employers which offer TSA's can find themselves in a pretty powerful investor position, especially if they employ many workers who are interested in the

plan. The range of investments open to the TSA-offering
employer is broad, and there is no reason why an organized
group of Progressive-minded employee-"shareholders" (like
yourself) in the plan shouldn't bring your influence to bear
in choosing investments that you deem socially desirable.

If you work for a for-profit company, look to see if they
offer (and if they don't suggest they do) a *salary reduction
plan.* Current law permits you to put up to 15 percent of your
earnings each year (until age 59½) into such a plan, which
is also tax- deferred as to both principal and the interest it
earns. You can't just withdraw the money tax-free, of
course—but you *can* do something you can't do with an IRA,
which is to pay tax on a lump-sum withdrawal as though
it were received in ten yearly installments of one-tenth each.
This ten-year averaging provision works to keep your tax
bracket down and can lead to some pretty good tax savings.

There are as many permutations and combinations of
these plans as there are people trying to sell them to you.
Discover them, investigate them and *use* them to your best
advantage—and that of the country.

3

Political Campaign Contributions—Splitting the Bill with Uncle Sam

"Who are to be the electors of the federal representatives? Not the rich, more than the poor; not the learned, more than the ignorant; not the haughty heirs of distinguished names, more than the humble sons of obscurity and unpropitious fortune. The electors are to be the great body of the people of the United States."

James Madison, in Federalist No. 7

"... the concept that government may restrict speech, i.e., spending of some elements of our society in order to enhance the relative voices of others is wholly foreign to the First Amendment."

The U.S. Supreme Court
Striking down Congressionally enacted campaign expenditure limits as unconstitutional in *Buckley v. Valeo* (1976)*

Make no mistake: running for office in these United States is a billion dollar business today. According to the Federal Elections Commission, successful primary candidates who ran for Congress spent $99 million total in the 1975-76 campaign season; just four years later, in 1979-80, the figure had more than doubled to $192 million.

If you want to be a U.S. Congressman, and your name isn't a household word, and you are not Robert Redford (or even a Redford look-alike), you will have to plan on raising and spending several hundred thousand dollars just to put on what the pro's would refer to as a "credible" candidacy. Now if you happen to be solidly pro-business in the positions

---

* Both quotes taken from "Big Bucks in Politics: Sin Against the Constitution," by the Hon. J. Skelly Wright, Judge of the U.S. Court of Appeals for the District of Columbia, *Washington Post*, October 31, 1982, Pp. C1-2.

you take, your biggest and surest source of funding is bound
to be a creature still relatively new to politics: the Political
Action Committee, or "PAC."

PACs In Control

PACs are, to many minds, the illegitimate offspring of the
post-Watergate "clean it up" cry. Originally seen as a means
of doing away with illegal corporate campaign contributions
to federal candidates, they have emerged instead as the
primary vehicle for special interests, especially business ones,
to maximize their political clout. Back at the end of 1974,
there were 608 PACs: 89 were affiliated with corporations,
201 with labor unions, and the rest with various other interests. As of mid-1982 *3,149* PACs had bloomed, with almost
half, 1,415 of them, belonging to business firms (of the rest,
only 350 were affiliated with labor).

Between the beginning of 1981 and the middle of
1982—with the '82 mid-term Congressional elections still five
months away—these PACs contributed more than $34
million to U.S. House and Senate contenders, more than 50
percent over their combined contributions for the equivalent
1979-80 period. The National Conservative Political Action
Committee was reported ready to raise and spend up to $10
million in support of office-seeker-adherents to its agenda;
PACs created by the oil and gas industry had already given
more than $3 million to their incumbent and challenger
friends between January '81 and May '82. Six years ago,
union-sponsored PACs regularly outraised and outspent
business ones. Today, by some estimates, business PACs
outspend their labor rivals three-to-one. And at the other end
of the legislative tunnel comes a steady flow of tales noting
how 83 percent of congressmen voting to kill a proposed auto
consumer-protection regulation got campaign money from
the car dealers' PAC; how eleven members receiving more
than $3,000 each from companies involved in the Clinch River
Breeder nuclear reactor project voted to continue its federal

financing (a ten-vote shift could have cut it off), and on, and on.

As you can see, a funny thing happened on the way to reform: those who got the most bucks to blow on a relative "luxury" good (or "business expense") like a political campaign, also got the upper hand. And what they are buying are, coincidentally, bodies-politic sharply in line with their way of thinking on economic matters, on defense and on federal regulatory involvement.

Evening The Score

The federal tax code offers individual income taxpayers an interesting and incredibly often overlooked opportunity to even that score somewhat. What it offers is a *political contributions credit*, and it works like this:

As Tom and Tammy Taxpayer, you're of modest means and have only modest inclination, if any, to financially support contenders for public office. Just the same, you decide you *can* afford to spend $50 a year, maximum, if just the right candidate comes along and hits you up just the right way. Stop right there: if you can *afford* to spend $50, set aside *$100* instead, *because Uncle Sam will match you dollar-for-dollar on the contributions you make.* In other words, if you give $100 this year, and then file your return indicating the contribution (or contributions) on your tax return, you will get a *tax credit* for one-half your contribution—you will get $50 back, leaving you with what you intended to spend max in the first place. And you will get this credit whether you itemize your deductions, or take the standard deduction.

There is a ceiling on this credit you need to be aware of. It's $50 for those filing singly (which means that the most you can contribute for which you'll get back half is $100), and $100 for joint returns (which means that the two of you can give up to $200 and get back half).

Remember that this ceiling is a per *year* limit, *not* a per *candidate* limit. So make that ceiling work to your advantage: if the House candidate you love is worth $400 of your joint support, don't give it *all* to him in his election year; give him $200 a year for two years running! Similarly, U.S. senators are up for re-election every six years. Assuming you're married, that means that you could support your favorite incumbent senator or senatorial candidate to the tune of $1,200 ($200 × six years) and *still* have Uncle Sam paying 50 percent of the total tab!

A couple of other bits of information about the political contributions credit are worth noting. First and foremost is that the candidates you choose to support are the candidates *you* choose: they can be incumbents or challengers; running for federal, state or local elective office; running in a primary or general election contest. Alternatively, your credit-eligible contribution can be made to an organization or committee organized exclusively to support one or more such candidates—this would include a PAC, for instance—or to a national, state or local committee of a national political party. But beware—if you buy a raffle ticket or similar item, although its designed to raise campaign funds, no credit.

Disclosure Isn't Required

Finally, using the tax credit does *not* mean that you are required to disclose the identity of the candidate or committee or party you gave to. It's still your First Amendment right to keep that information to yourself, unless, of course, your overall contribution was over the limit that triggers disclosure requirements under the federal election law, or election code of your state or locality. And of course, there is no credit for direct contributions to the Presidential candidates of the major political parties because such contributions can't lawfully be made, thanks to public funding of Presidential campaigns.

Presidential Fund Checkoff

How does this public funding work? Again, it's a creature of the post-Watergate campaign-reform movement, and it appears as though it's here to stay. If we as citizens believe that a fully enlightened citizenry makes the best electorate, then we have to believe that a certain threshold amount of public Presidential campaign financing equal to both sides (and perhaps to a third-party contender), is a good thing *per se*. And if we believe that, we have to start checking a tiny, hard-to-notice, insignificant-looking box on our tax returns—it doesn't even merit a line number—called the *Presidential Election Campaign Fund Checkoff*.

If you check "yes" on this box, it means that $1 of your taxes paid will be taken out of the general fund and placed instead in the Presidential election campaign fund; if you check "no," then no dollar is allocated. If you check neither box, no money is allocated—there is no "presumed civic spirit" when it comes to tax allocations, none at all.

Remember—it costs *you* nothing to check off a dollar for the fund—but it does take one dollar away from the general fund. And it does help to support our right to an ample airing of presidential politics every four years.

4

Buying a Home

Home's not merely four square walls
Though with pictures hung and guilded;
Home is where Affection calls,—
Filled with shrines the Heart hath builded.

Charles Swain (1803—1874)

Only ten percent of the American population can afford a home today, according to one trade group's figures, down from fully 40 percent merely ten years ago. The average new American home now costs a staggering $93,000. At the end of 1982, 143,000 homeowners across the nation were involved in a foreclosure proceeding, according to the Mortgage Bankers Association. One of every 17 homeowners is 30 days or more past due on a payment, and in some parts of the country the number of delinquency notices almost equals the number of homes being sold. Of course the latter fact is the result of dismal sales as well as soaring delinquencies: with conventional mortgage rates still well into the teens, unloading a house is an event worthy of celebration.

Clearly, if owning one's home is as American as apple pie, someone or something is making the crust go stale. With sudden unemployment still more than a distant possibility to more working Americans than at anytime since the 1930's, fiscal caution is the watchword, and homeownership is one of those luxuries put off till less tumultuous times return. Of course, the flip-side of the less-homebuying coin is the tightest residential rental market the country has seen in years; in the Los Angeles-Orange County area, the 1982 vacancy rate hovered at around 1.8 percent, and a region is considered lucky these days if vacancies top five percent.

Should You Buy A Home?

What does all this apparently overwhelming evidence of gloom and doom say to the moderate-income Progressive-minded taxpayer?

Buy a home, *now*. But do it right.

This advice is respectfully offered subject to the following reasoning:

• The steadily skyhigh interest rates we have lived with for several years now, created a buyer's market generally for housing, and, in some cases, "distress sale" bargains that in healthier economic times simply would not exist.

• Those same interest rates spawned a hydra-like creature known as "creative financing," which can make it possible for you to buy a home—maybe not your dream home, but an appreciating stepping-stone to that dream home— for a much smaller monthly payment than you might expect.

• Those same high interest rates, as we'll see, have resulted in Uncle Sam picking up more and more of the cost of residential housing. You as a renting *taxpayer* have to help shoulder that cost, so you may as well benefit from it as a homeowning *taxsaver* as well.

• There are precautions you can take to "shield" yourself and your family against losing your home by reason of unemployment.

• If you can buy your home at a "cheap" price now (because of high interest and hard-up sellers) and economic times improve, you will have a much-appreciated asset on your hands.

Some of these arguments are self explanatory; others deserve a more detailed discussion.

How Much of a Home Can You Afford?

That's the critical first question you should be asking yourself. The experts have several rules-of-thumb for answering it. One is that the cost of the home you buy should not exceed two-and-one-half times your annual gross household income; if you and your spouse earn a combined $35,000 a year before taxes, then stop looking at homes with price tags beyond $87,500. A second rule-of-thumb is that your monthly mortgage payment ought not exceed 28-33 percent of your combined gross monthly income; so if you earn a combined $1,000 every two weeks, then stop looking at homes which would carry monthly payments above $670.

These rules should tell you something quite elementary about buying a home: the higher the price, the less likely you can afford it. But what these rules also tend to ignore are the tax consequences of *how* you buy your home, and how those consequences can put a home appearing to be too expensive back within your range of affordability.

Hidden Low-Interest Subsidies

What makes this especially true today are the subsidized low interest mortgage rates many nervous builders and anxious homesellers are offering to attract would-be buyers. These below-market financing breaks are often "capitalized" and added on in some fashion to the price of the home when you buy it. Therefore, as Washington D.C. real estate expert Kenneth Harney explains it, "What would otherwise be a deductible item for buyers—their interest expense—is converted instead into a non-deductible capital item." Harney offered the readers of his regular column in the *Washington Post* a formula created by Kansas City tax attorney Ernest Fleischer to see how subsidized interest rates translate into a "padded" house price. Fleischer figures that for each percentage point of subsidy of the interest rate provided by the builder, the selling price may be adjusted upward by seven percent over what the property's true evaluation would be in an all-cash (or market-rate interest) sale. (This rule figures the "present value" of the annual rate subsidy in a market where the prevailing interest rate is 15 percent, over a 12 year period.)

Harney then offers the following illustration of this formula at work:

"If the cash value of a home were $100,000, in other words, a builder who bought down the long-term fixed rate of a purchaser six months ago by three points—say from 16 to 13 percent—might have sold the house for about $120,000. The padding of the rate discount onto the true cash price probably wouldn't have been disclosed. Federal truth-in-lending regulations don't require it. What looked like a good deal on the rate to the buyer six months ago, however, doesn't look quite as attractive in light of today's falling rates. Mortgages with adjustable-rate features are readily available in the 13 percent range or below. They cost little or nothing in extra capital outlays up front.

"The buyers paid a price inflated by 20 percent to compensate for the cost of long-term capital in a 16 percent market. The $20,000 up-front interest-rate premium can't be deducted on the buyers' taxes, however, because it was never labeled as interest. It can't be written off, nor can the buyer refinance the deal to "wash out" the excess cost of money he's built in. In today's market, the $20,000 would be hard to recover in the event of a quick resale. Had the buyer pushed the builder harder on price—and calculated the padding he was getting stuck with—he probably could have ended up closer to the $100,000 cash value of the property. He might have had a slightly higher mortgage rate—all tax deductible—but avoided the non-deductible financing premium he paid. Most likely he would have also limited his down payment to around $10,000 (at the $100,000 price), rather than having to pay $30,000 to qualify for the same size loan (but on a house priced at $120,000). The extra $20,000 in down payment could have been working for him today in an investment, ideally a tax-exempt security yielding 14 percent or higher. Instead, his $20,000 is working against him, and may even result in higher local property-tax assessments."

Equity Sharing

There is another way to increase the value of the home you can afford, and this method, steadily gaining in popularity everywhere, is known as "equity sharing." What makes equity sharing work so well in some situations is that it marries the would-be owner-occupier's needs with those of a would-be real-estate investor—and that's one marriage that the current tax laws heavily favor.

Here's how it works.

Assume you have your eye on a $62,000 home. The 14½ percent conventional mortgage you can obtain with a 10 percent downpayment would leave you a monthly payment of about $750 PITI (Principal + Interest + Property Taxes + Insurance). Now that immediately creates two problems for you: you don't have enough for the $6,200 downpayment, and you're not sure you can *really* afford that monthly payment.

Here's where the hero of the day, your equity partner, jumps into the picture. Most likely this person fits one of two categories: he is a close relative, perhaps your father-in-law, who wants to see you settled into a productive investment. Or he is a regular real-estate investor whose name's been given to the real-estate agent handling the home you're interested in.

Now here's one common way in which the equity partnership would work. *Each* of you puts up *one-half* the down payment—$3,100 apiece. *Each* of you would put up *one-half* the costs associated with buying the house (so-called "settlement costs"). Both of you would settle upon a current market rental value for the property—let's call it $450 a month. Now. because you and your partner are 50-50 co-owners of the property—and you live there and he doesn't—you treat him, in effect, like "one-half a landlord." That is, you pay him one-half the rent every month, or $225. But because you and your partner are 50-50 owners, you *each* owe one-half the monthly payment of $750, or $375 apiece. In sum, *your* monthly expenses under an equity partnership now come to $375 (monthly payment) + $225 (half the rent) = $600, $150 *less* than your monthly payment as the sole owner. *Your partner's* monthly costs, on the other hand, are $375 (monthly payment) −$225 (your rent to him) = $150.

It's the *tax consequences* of equity partnerships that make them truly attractive. You, as the owner-occupier, still receive tax deductions for a variety of items the tax laws permit to purchasers of their own homes. You can deduct various costs associated with the purchase itself—so-called "settlement" costs, including fees paid to the lender, title search fees and transfer taxes, and others (see your settlement attorney for an exact list). You receive a deduction for your one-half share of the yearly property taxes. And of course, the big one: you are entitled to deduct that part of your $375 monthly payment which constitutes the interest payment on your mortgage. You don't have any deduction for the $225 "rent" you pay your partner every month, but your out-of-pocket monthly costs have been reduced almost that much anyway.

For your partner, the tax considerations are wholly different. He must declare as ordinary income the $225 rent he gets from you every month. But from his perspective, remember, your home constitutes "income property," thereby opening up to him tax advantages not available to you.

Against his income he can set off the expenses associated with owning and managing the property—his share of the deductible settlement costs and mortgage interest and property taxes, plus his share of insurance, and maintenance (if he contributes to it under your partnership agreement). And then your partner gets *his* big one: a deduction for "depreciation" attributable to his half-ownership in the house.

Depreciation?

It is depreciation, beyond anything else, that makes the world of real-estate investment go 'round. Depreciation is a device in the tax law which permits you to assume that an asset you own which you use in your business, or hold for the production of income, will be "used up" over the course of its life. This assumption may well make sense for tables and chairs, airplanes and cars, which do ultimately wear out—but it's always a wonder why it should also apply to *real estate* which always seems to go *up* in value over time . . . . and up, and up. The point is, it does apply—not to land, but to the structures built upon the land; and not to owner-occupied residences, but to any other business-related or income-producing real estate. The discussion which follows applies to real estate investments generally, and to your equity-partner in particular.

In this case, the purchase price of the property is $62,000. Let's assume that, of that total price, the portion allocatable to (non-depreciable) land value is $20,000; subtract that amount, and we're left with $42,000 as the value of the building itself. Divide by half, and we come up with $21,000 as the property's value subject to depreciation by your partner—its depreciable *basis,* in the jargon of the trade.

The next question is obvious: what's the "life" of the property? Until very recently, different kinds of property were assigned very different "useful lives." In the case of investment residential real estate a typical useful life could have been 30 to 40 years. The 1981 Economic Recovery Tax Act changed all that by establishing a much narrower range of "recovery periods" for different categories of property; for most forms of "real property" (real estate, like rental housing), the recovery period set by law is 15 years.

Your partner now has a choice, the same choice he would have with regard to any real estate investment made in 1982 or thereafter. He could choose to depreciate the property "straight line"; that is, to take a deduction for one-fifteenth of $21,000 for each of the next 15 years. Each year in which he does so, his basis in the property will be *adjusted downward* by the amount of depreciation taken. Thus, at the end of Year 1 of your joint ownership of the house, your partner would be eligible to take a deduction of $\frac{1}{15} \times \$21,000 = \$1,400$, and the house's adjusted basis would become $\$21,000 - \$1,400 = \$19,600$. Now, were he to *sell* his share in the property right at the beginning of Year 2, let's say for $23,000, his profit on the sale for tax purposes would be, not just the $2,000 he receives over what he paid, but $2,000 *plus* the $1,400 of depreciation he had already taken. But note how that profit is taxed: *all of it,* including the $1,400, is taxed as *capital gains* income; that is, at 40 percent of your partner's ordinary income tax rate. By taking "straight line" depreciation, your partner has set up a classic "conversion"-style tax shelter for himself. He's succeeded in "converting" $1,400 of income from income taxed at ordinary income rates, into income taxed at preferred capital gains rates. He's also succeeded in creating a "deferral"-type tax shelter for himself, by deferring having to pay any tax on $1,400 of income from the time he took the depreciation, until the time he sold his share in the house. Hence, the magic of depreciation.

Accelerated Depreciation

But it gets even better. Under the 1981 tax law, your partner doesn't have to be satisfied with taking his depreciation "straight line," i.e., in equal increments over the 15-year recovery period. He can *accelerate* his depreciation, employing something called the "Accelerated Cost Recovery System" ("ACRS") to take the lion's share of the depreciation he's entitled to during the earliest years of ownership. In fact, under ACRS he may take as much as 12 percent of his $21,000 basis—$2,500—at the end of his first year of ownership. And then, ACRS will still permit him to *switch back* to straight-line depreciation later on, when that method would increase his deduction! The double-magic of accelerated depreciation is that it enhances the "deferral" aspect of the tax shelter substantially. But be careful: it does *not* normally enhance the "conversion" aspect over "straight line." That's because any depreciation your partner takes using the accelerated method, which is in excess of what he would have been allowed to take under the "straight line" method, will ultimately be "recaptured" *as ordinary income, not capital gains,* when he sells the property. That may not matter to your partner, especially if he expects to be in a substantially lower tax bracket when he sells out; but he could be in for a sizzling tax sting if his bracket is up substantially, or even stays where it is now, at the time of sale.

So much for the tax consequences of your equity partnership. Note, of course, that you and your partner are each 50 percent co-owners of the property. Any document setting forth your respective ownership rights and responsibilities with respect to the home must be prepared with great care, preferably by an attorney fully familiar with the in's and out's of equity partnerships. But it's well worth every minute of effort if it will put you into your own home.

Homesharing

Another animal with some of the characteristics of equity partnerships, but not all, is *homesharing*. Homesharing involves buying your home with another *owner-occupier*. The 50-50 splitting arrangement is much the same as for an equity partnership, but here, of course, your partner is more than your partner—he (or she) is your housemate. Personal compatibility becomes an issue that it never was in the equity partnership. Second, because both of you are owner-occupiers, neither of you will qualify for those tax deductions associated with real estate investment but not homeownership that we've just reviewed.

Simultaneous Homeownership And Investment

A third variation involves you becoming both homeowner and investor at the same time. This can be accomplished essentially three ways: (1) by buying a multi-unit property, such as a duplex, and renting out one of the units; (2) by converting an appropriate space in your single-family home into a separate rental unit; or (3) by turning a part of your house into an office or other place of business. Let's look briefly at these options.

Rental Units

Buying a duplex, and converting a portion of your single-family dwelling into rental space, accomplish essentially the same thing: each turns a portion of your residence into "income property," triggering a set of tax consequences of great importance to you. Furthermore, under a recent change in the tax laws your tenant may be a parent or a child—it doesn't matter, for tax purposes, so long as rent actually changes hands, and is set at fair market value. That portion of your property that is attributable to rental acquires the same tax-characteristics as any other residential income property—it becomes "depreciable," and—although you must include the rents you earn as ordinary income—the costs associated with maintaining that part of the home and other "rental expenses" become tax-deductible costs to you. In sum, the net after-tax effects of renting out some part of your dwelling could make your house a substantially more affordable undertaking. And given the near-nationwide housing shortage, you'll also be doing your community a favor.

In-Home Office Or Business

Allocating a portion of your home to an office or business can also have its tax advantages, but here lie several traps for the unwary. The rules are complicated and it is wise to seek personalized tax advice before converting part of your home to business use, but there is one general rule to know. You may treat those expenses attributable to the business use of your home as tax-deductible, *only* to the extent that this portion of the home is used *exclusively*, and *on a regular basis*, as your *principal place of business, or* as *a place of business which you use in the normal course of business to meet with patients, clients or customers.* Now let's define the italicized terms. "Exclusively" means just what it says: a specific part of the home must be set aside for business use *only*. If your den doubles as a study, forget it; likewise if your kids use the couch in your basement office to watch TV nights. "On a regular basis" is a test *in addition to,* not in place of, the "exclusive" test. Occasional or incidental use of the business area isn't going to be good enough—you must really work there. "Principal place" of business need not mean the *only place*, however. If you're self-employed, it should be your "headquarters," not a second office away from the main office. If you are someone else's employee, you can still have your "principal place of business" in your home, but only if, in addition to meeting all the other conditions, you can demonstrate that it is *to your employer's convenience* that your office be in your home. (This would be true, for instance, for a regional columnist of a national magazine whose employer's base of operations is half-way around the country.) Of course, if you have a second business that you run out of your home, separate from, but in addition to your day-time work, these tests can be satisfied by that second business alone.

There are two exceptions to the "exclusive use" rule. One is for retail salesmen who store their goods at home; that space need not be used "exclusively" for that purpose, but it must still be "separately identifiable" (i.e., the attic) and used on a regular basis.

In-Home Day Care Center

The second exception is much more interesting. If you wish to provide a day care service, and get a state license to do so, you may treat the costs of providing the service as tax-deductible regardless of whether any part of your home was used exclusively for the service or not. "Day care services" are defined as "qualified day care services provided to children, persons aged 65 or older, or those physically or mentally incapable of caring for themselves." Before we take an example based on the above exception, one warning: the amount of deductions you may take for the business use of your home *in any case*, is limited to no more than the gross income derived from business use of the home, less the allocable portion of the usual home-related tax deductions (mortgage interest and property taxes).

Now let's look at an example. Suppose, Tammy Taxpayer, that while Tom is out laboring to earn enough money to pay the monthly mortgage on your new home, you start a daytime day care service for working mothers. Let's assume you've chosen not to seek work outside the home for a couple of years because you've just had your own child. So from nine to five every weekday, the kids of other working mothers stay with you. You charge for the service, and over a year, your gross income comes to $6,000.

Now let's say that your total monthly mortgage payment is $650, of which $600 is mortgage interest. That brings your total yearly interest payments to $600 × 12 = $7200. Add your annual real estate taxes of $1,800 to get $9,000 regularly tax-deductible, home-related expenses.

Now let's pretend, for a moment, that your *entire* home were to qualify as "investment real estate" which you rent out, i.e., use to produce income, *all the time*. As you've seen already, you would have additional tax-deductible expenditures, such as maintenance, insurance and depreciation. Let's assume you calculate those costs in their entirety, and they come to $7,200 over the same year.

The next step is easy. You've already determined that the time your home is devoted to "business use," i.e., your day care service, is 8 hrs/day × 5 days/week × 50 weeks a year = 2,000 hours a year. What fraction of the *total* "use" of your home is that business use? "Total" business use would be 24 hrs/day × 7 days/week × 52 weeks a year = 8,736 hours a year (the total number of hours in a year!). Now divide 2,000 by 8,736 to get .23, the fraction of total-use-time

that your home is devoted to your day-care service. The rest
of the calculations go like this:

1. Gross income from day-care service.....................$6,000.
2. Less the allocable normal home-related tax deductions:
   $9,000 × .23...$2,070.
3. Limit on remaining deductible expenses:
   Line 1 minus Line 2.................................$3,930.
4. Deductible expenses of home business use:
   (The smaller of actual expenses
   ($7200 × .23 = $1656) or line 3)...............$1656.

In other words, you have generated an additional $1,656
worth of tax deductions through the part-time use of your
home as a day care center. What's the entire effort worth
to you? Well, if you and Tom are in the 35 percent marginal
tax bracket, your $6,000 of extra income will become about
$3,900 after taxes, and your extra $1,656 in deductions will
be worth $580 in reduced taxes, for a combined $4,480 more
money *in your pocket*. That's more than half your mortgage
payments for the whole year! Not bad, Tammy, considering
you planned to spend the year at home in the first place!
That's called using the tax laws to your own advantage, and
to society's advantage too.

There is another important point to the duplex, rental-
unit and business-in-the-home illustrations, which goes back
to one of the main reasons you may be reluctant to buy a
home in these fiscal hard times: fear of sudden unemployment. Note how each of these devices would help *insulate*
you against the sudden shock of joblessness—in each case,
you would have a *second source* of funds with which to help
make that payment while you re-group to find new work.

The Well-Shielded Investment

There is another, wholly separate reason why buying a
home is such a good investment taxwise—and it has to do
with when it comes time to *sell*. Perhaps no investment is

as well shielded from the rabid bite of the taxman as one's primary residence. There are seven basic shields:

Shield One—The Residential Replacement Rule

Suppose you bought your home three years ago for $45,000. Since then your family has grown and you feel it's time to step up to a bigger (and naturally more expensive) place. You put your home on the market at an asking price of $60,000 and—low and behold—it *sells*. Now, if this were a piece of investment real estate, you would be confronted with a $15,000 taxable "profit." (This assumes for simplicity sake that no depreciation was taken on the property— you've already seen the tax implications on sale of depreciation above.) But this is your own, "principal residence," and so the Congress has bestowed upon its owner-occupier a special "residence replacement rule": you may *defer* paying taxes on all of that profit if, within 24 months of the sale of your principal residence, you purchase another principal residence of equal or greater cost. If your replacement-home costs *less*, then the difference in prices—up to the amount of your sale profits—is still taxable.*

Note two important features of the "residence replacement rule": first of all, the 24-month "window" applies to the period *before or after* the sale of your home; in other words, you don't have to wait until the first home sells to buy the second one. You must also occupy your replacement residence within this 24-month period.

Second, the rule doesn't eliminate the tax on your profits—it *defers* it. But that deferral will stick so long as you keep your second home, or trade up to a third one, a fourth one, and so on . . . *or* take advantage of Shield Two.

---

* However, you can also choose to take that difference in prices and apply it to reconstructing or remodeling your replacement home—and defer the profits this way too. But these costs must be for permanent improvements or replacements that extend the value and useful life of the house; mere repairs or fix-up costs don't qualify.

Shield Two—The Once-A-Lifetime Exclusion

You've deferred paying taxes on quite a few consecutive principal homes now. You're over 55 years old now, and feel it's time to sell and move into a rental apartment. So here's Shield Two: the one-time exclusion for an older person. Once during your lifetime, you can sell your home and take your profits out *tax-free*. This rule has several important characteristics. First of all, either you (or your spouse, if you file your taxes jointly) must be age 55 or older. Second, the exclusion is a once-a-lifetime privilege for the husband and wife *together*; if *either one* has taken it, even prior to marrying the other, the couple may not take it again. Third, the exclusion applies, in the case of a home sold after July 20, 1981, to gains up to $125,000 (or $62,500 in the case of a married taxpayer filing separately). (For pre-July 20 sales the figures are $100,000 and $50,000, respectively.) Fourth, you must have actually lived in your home, and treated it as your principal residence, for a total of at least three years during the past five years (a provision designed to avoid taxpayers using the exclusion for income property masquerading as primary residential property). Fifth, where the home in question has been used partially for income-generating purposes— like the duplex, rental-basement and home-office situations we discussed above—only that portion attributable to your principal residence will qualify for the one-time exclusion. Last, the one-time exclusion is an *option*, not a mandatory requirement. If you're over 55 and plan on *buying another* home, it's up to you whether you defer your profits using Shield One, or take the once-a-lifetime exclusion under Shield Two.

It's important to note that Shields One and Two can be coupled if the taxpayer is over 55, and his/her gain exceeds the $125,000 limit. Let's say you, Tom and Tammy, sell your home for $180,000. You had paid $35,000 for the property 20 years ago. In the process of preparing it for sale you incurred "fix up" costs of $1,000, and the real estate broker's sales commission comes to $9,000. Both costs can (generally) be subtracted from the sales price to leave you a "recognized gain" of $180,000 − $35,000 − $10,000 = $135,000. Tom's over 55, so he used his one-time exclusion to exclude $125,000 of those profits. That would still leave you both with $10,000 of "recognized gain" for tax purposes. Another way to look at the same figures would be to say that the "revised adjusted sales price" of Tom's home is its original $35,000 cost plus the recognized gain of $10,000 = $45,000. Now, if Tom buys a replacement home costing $45,000 or more, the recognized $10,000 gain will also be protected through deferral under the residence-replacement rule of Shield One.

Shield Three—Offsetting Sale-Related Costs

Shield Three was actually just glossed over above. When you sell a home, you usually put some cash into minor repairs and cosmetic improvements to make it more attractive to potential buyers. Those costs may be used to "offset" the sales price of your home—which serves to lower your recognized gain—provided: (1) they are not otherwise deducted (i.e., as business expenses); (2) they are not permanent, "capital improvements" which for tax purposes would be added to the "cost" of your house (and would serve to lower your gain that way); (3) they are paid for within 30 days after the sale of your home, and (4) the work was done no more than 90 days before the day the sales contract for your house was signed. Similarly, the commission you pay your real-estate broker can be offset against the sales price.

Shield Four—Installment Sales

No law says that when you sell your home, or any other property for that matter, you must accept full payment from the buyer on the date of sale. In fact, with commercially-offered mortgage interest rates out of reach of more and more potential buyers, a new form of "creative financing" known as the "installment sale" is becoming steadily more popular. And there are important tax benefits available to the installment homeseller too. Suppose that during the year in which you plan to sell your home, your other income is substantial enough to put you in the 50 percent tax bracket (or suppose, alternatively, that the year following the year in which you sell your home you plan to retire, and have only negligible income). By selling your house in an installment sale, you can defer tax-recognition of your "profits" until the year in which the buyer *actually pays you* the installments. Let's assume you sell your house (for which you originally paid $90,000) for $180,000, and let's further assume that you don't have any sale costs to pay, so your actual profit is $90,000, a 100 percent gain. If you don't plan to buy another home, and aren't 55 years old, then Shields One and Two aren't available to you and you're facing having to fork over a hefty slice of your $90,000 to Uncle Sam in capital gains tax. Now suppose instead that you agree with the buyer to take a $45,000 down payment at the time of sale, and "carry" the remaining $135,000 for three years, at 10 percent interest, with principal payments of $45,000 being made in each of those years. Because your profit upon sale was 100 percent, it is assumed for tax purposes that one-half of each $45,000 installment payment is profit, and you will owe capital gains tax on $22,500 each of those years. You will also owe tax at higher, ordinary income rates, on the 10 percent interest you're going to be paid during the remaining pay periods. But given that your marginal bracket will be substantially less in years 2-4 (as we assumed), *and* given that your "profit" income will be only $22,500 in each of those years (versus $90,000 in a single year), the overall amount of taxes you'll pay through an installment sale can be substantially less than what you would have had to pay in a lump-sum sale.

Shield Five—Swapping

No law says that if you want your neighbor's house more than your own, you have to *sell* yours and *buy* hers—you can *swap*. And if you do, not only will you save real estate commissions and many other costs associated with real estate transactions, but you'll save tax payments too. At least, you'll *defer* the taxes you owe, because your "profits" will be reflected in an adjustment to the basis of the home you swap for. The effect is much the same as that under the residence-replacement rule of Shield One.

Shield Six—Gifts

You want to sell your house and move into a rental apartment, but if you do—because you're not yet 55—you face paying taxes of, let's say, $10,000, on your $50,000 profit. Purely by coincidence, your eldest son is about to marry the ravishing daughter of the richest doctor in town, and you want to give the couple a wedding gift that will set the town gossipmongers afire.

Give them your house. Uncle Sam will gladly share in the gift.

We'll talk more about the magic of gift-giving later on. But recognize, for now, that the principles apply to real estate as well as to any other form of tangible property. Whatever the basis of your home was at the time of the gift, becomes the basis in the hands of your son and daughter-in-law; when *they* sell, *your* $10,000 profit will be taxable (along with any additional profit) to them. (But then, why should they care— you've given them a free house!) The taxman will look closely at several aspects of the transaction to justify calling it a bona-fide "gift." First, you must be "competent" to make the gift. Second, your son must be capable of receiving it. Third, there must be clear evidence that you "clearly and unmistakably" intend to make the gift: to divest of yourself of title, to give up all "dominion and control" over the property, immediately, absolutely and irrevocably. In other words, don't even think about using Shield Six unless you *really mean it*. Fourth, you must actually give up title and deliver the property to the donee (the couple), who must clearly accept it.

Stop right there. You've heard that there's another animal in the tax code called the gift tax. And with a gift this big, you're worried about the prospect of a wallop in the wallet from this unexpected other corner. The gift tax is explored in greater detail in Chapter 11; suffice it to say, for now, that unless you make *other* substantial gifts to this couple or to others, totaling tens of thousands of dollars, you won't have to worry about the gift tax (as the law is presently written) playing any role in this particular transaction. So relax.

Shield Seven—Transfer At Death

Finally, you can take what is in many ways the most tax-advantaged course, and clearly the meanest to Uncle Sam: you can hold onto the property and leave it to somebody in your will. The tax laws contain a unique feature pertaining to property passed by inheritance, and it's called the "step up in basis rule." What the rule says, simply, is that no matter what your basis was in the property at the time of your death, it acquires a *completely new basis equal to its fair market value at the time of inheritance.* To illustrate: let's say you paid $50,000 for your home, made no capital improvements, and the day before you die, you'd be able to sell for $150,000. You would have recognized a "profit" (assuming no other shields apply) of $100,000, with a heavy capital gains taxbite thereon. But if your wife inherits the house, its present market value still being $150,000, its basis is magically transformed—"stepped up"—to $150,000. Your $100,000 in profit has been lost to Uncle Sam forever! In other words, should your wife then sell the home for $200,000, she would be taxed solely on $50,000 profit.

The seven shields of prudent homeselling should suggest something to you pretty strongly. If you're *even thinking* about selling, sit down with your tax advisor and work through all the tax considerations *first*. You'll be amazed at the extent to which Uncle Sam has gone to make buying and selling a home a tax-preferred investment to end *all* investments.

5

Residential Energy Credits—The High-Power Tax Break

It's shortly before New Years. You're ensconced at the dining room table, a mountain of unsorted credit-card receipts fighting for your attention as you gaze sleepily out into the snowy garden and ponder how the hell you'll be able to pay next month's fuel bill.

This is precisely the time, Tom and Tammy Taxpayer, to *start* thinking about how much taxes you are going to save *next* year—and how much in heating and cooling costs—by improving the energy-efficiency of your home, and/or converting to a different source of energy.

Now if you rent your residence, don't stop reading—you *don't* have to own the place you live in, to take advantage of this tax shelter; in fact, there may be some real savings in store for you if you do rent, and have a landlord who's willing to listen to some creative quick talking. Read on, renter, read on.

This chapter will talk about two types of *residential energy tax credits*. The first is available for a wide range of activities that *conserve* the amount of energy you use in your home. The second is available for a selected group of energy-*producing* innovations that increase your home's dependence on *renewable* energy sources, namely solar, wind and geothermal power, and lower its reliance on non-renewable fuels like oil, natural gas and coal.

But before we get into the mechanics of the residential energy credits, let's look quickly at some interesting statistics. Since 1978, the year the credits came into effect, about 15.5 million individual income tax returns have been filed claiming one or both credits in some amount.*

That number may sound large, but in comparison with the overall number of returns filed it's not. In fact, in 1980 (the most recent year for which figures are available) only 4.7 million returns out of a total of 93.9 million filed—just one in 20—claimed the credit. But even the small number who did claim it, reported spending nearly $3.65 billion on energy-conservation and renewable-energy items in 1980, and *were able, through the credits, to reduce their federal 1980 income taxes by $562 million.*

Now here's what the credits are, and how they work. Because the inner workings of the conservation and renewable-source credits are different, we'll treat them separately.

Conservation Tax Credits

Here we are again dealing with a tax *credit* as opposed to a tax *deduction*. Remember the crucial distinction: a deduction is an offset against your taxable income, and what it's worth to you personally depends upon your tax bracket: the higher your bracket, the more it's worth. A tax credit, in contrast, is *insensitive* to what your income-tax bracket is, because it is an offset against the taxes you actually owe. In other words, a one- dollar credit is *always* worth more than a one-dollar deduction—but whether a one-dollar credit is worth more than a *$2.50* deduction depends on how much *you* earn.

The credit is available for conservation-related expenditures made on the "principal U.S. residence" of any taxpayer, provided that the residence in question was "substantially completed" before April 20, 1977. What sort of expenditures qualify?

---

* These and other figures are drawn from Thompson, Richard, and Hillelson, Rich, "Residential Energy Credit, 1978-1980," *Statistics of Income Bulletin*, Washington, D.C.; Internal Revenue Service, Fall, 1982, Pp. 1-8.

• *Insulation*: Insulation is defined as "any item specifically and primarily designed to reduce the heat loss or gain" of the home itself, or of the water-heater in the home.

• *Other "energy-conserving components"*: One major group of "components" consists of improvements to a *furnace*: for instance, a replacement of your furnace burner which is more energy-efficient than the original burner; any device which modifies the output of your heating system or its fuel opening, so as to increase its "efficiency" (for instance, a damper which allows selective heating or cooling of certain rooms at a time); and an electrical or mechanical furnace ignition system which replaces a gas pilot light (which unnecessarily burns gas). A second group pertains to *insulation-related improvements*: storm and thermal windows and doors; caulking or weatherstripping of an exterior door or window. And a third group consists of *other energy-saving devices*, such as thermostats with built-in timers that turn heating and cooling systems down during certain parts of the day, or meters which display energy-usage.

How The Conservation Credit Works

So long as the work is done on your principal U.S. residence, Tom and Tammy, whether you own it or rent it, a tax credit is available for *15 percent of up to $2,000* spent during the tax year on the kinds of things listed above, *up to a maximum credit of $300*. Note—not just the cost of *materials* (windows, caulking, etc.) qualifies for the credit, but the cost of *labor* associated with installing those materials too, provided of course that you hire a licensed professional and don't do the work yourself.

A quick example. First, suppose you've spent $1,700 during the year on new thermal windows, and an additional $200 to have them installed. Comes tax time, you've calculated your federal income taxes owed for the year at $1,400.

First, add the cost of materials to the cost of labor: $1,700 + $200 = $1,900. Divide by 15 percent to get the amount of the tax credit: $1,900 × .15 = $285. That $285 is your actual tax savings, because instead of owing $1,400, you now owe only $1,400 − $285 = $1,115.

Now suppose, instead, that you spent what it says you spent above, and in addition you installed a replacement-burner for your furnace which cost you $500 to buy and $75 to install. Add the two costs to get $575, and add this to your prior energy-conservation total of $1,900 to get $2,475. Oh, oh—look what you've done. You didn't take the *ceiling* on the conservation credit into account when you made that second purchase! That ceiling is $300 for the credit itself; or calculating backwards, because the credit is for 15 percent of what you spend, then $2,000 is the most you can spend on energy conservation *on this principal residence* as long as you, Tom and Tammy Taxpayer, are the owners of it, and still remain *completely* eligible for the credit. In this example, the taxpayer still gains only $300 in credits, and won't be able to take any additional energy-conservation tax credits until the day she purchases a new principal residence, and makes credit-qualified conservation expenditures on it. Hence, the maxim you heard first in the introduction: to work, *taxsaving must be a year-round way-of-life, not an April 15th afterthought.*

Note one important thing about this credit: it's almost as if you bought your energy-conservation stuff at a 15 percent-off sale. Smart retailers and contractors know that, and many have instituted price increases which in effect "cancel out" the tax savings. So be careful when you purchase your supplies—remember, it's *you* who Uncle Sam is trying to reward, not the salesman across the counter.

Some Technical Rules

There are some important technical rules about this energy-conservation tax credit you need to be aware of. Here's the list:

• As we said, the residence on which you make the energy improvements must have been "substantially completed" before April 20, 1977. (Don't ask why, because you really don't care. Just make sure, Tom and Tammy Tax*planner*, that if you're scouting around for a house to buy and find one that needs thousands in energy-efficiency improvements—check out when it was built.)

• The credit is available for items installed in or on the residence after April 20, 1977, and before January 1, 1986. But remember, with the exception of the next rule below, only expenditures made during the tax year are eligible for a credit in that particular year. Also you, the taxpayer, must be the first to make use of the improvement you've made. Also, the property must be expected to remain in use at least three years.

• The income tax credit for energy-conservation expenditures is *nonrefundable*—that is, if the credit exceeds your taxes owed, you will not receive a check for the additional balance—i.e., a positive subsidy—from the government. But if the amount of the credit you're eligible for exceeds the amount in taxes you owe, you *don't* lose the balance. Instead, you may "carry it over," that is, apply it to taxes you will owe in future years. So, for instance, if you owe $250 in federal income taxes this year and your credit comes to $300, when you get around to paying your taxes next year remember to subtract $50 from what you owe then. There's an important lesson to be learned here: detailed recordkeeping of all taxes paid is *essential* if you are going to benefit to the maximum from all the tax-sheltering devices available to you. There is one restriction on this carryover provision: it is limited to tax years ending before 1988.

• The credit is available to homeowners, and renters, and those who own shares in a cooperative housing association or are members of a condominium management association. So if you live in a coop or condo, and read in your association's newsletter about some energy-saving plans for your building that are down the road, better make sure that someone wielding power on the board of directors knows all about tax credits for energy conservation.

• To claim a credit, it must amount to at least $10. That is, your energy-conservation related expenditures in any tax-year must be at least $67.

• Unfortunately for all of us, the $300 ceiling on the credit is *not* an annual limit on what *you* can take, but an accumulated "forever" limit for *your principal residence*. In other words, if you make $2,000 worth of improvements on the apartment you rent, and take the full $300 credit, that is the maximum energy-conservation credit *allowed to you for that apartment*. This little-appreciated fact presents an important tax-planning element, once again, for the homehunter: if you find a place which you think could stand thousands (or even hundreds) in energy-improvements, make sure to ask the owner *whether the energy-conservation tax credit for that particular property has already been taken, in part or in full*. It could be worth up to $300 to you to know.

• If the conservation-related improvement you've made is a "capital improvement"—such as a new set of storm windows, for example—you will want to add the cost to the "basis" of your home for purposes of reducing your recognized taxable gain when you sell (see Page 66). You can do so in this case, too, but *only* to the extent of the improvement's price that does not come right back to you in the form of the credit.

• If any part of your energy-conservation improvement expenditure was fully or partially financed by a non-taxable government grant or other form of government subsidy . . . . sorry. *That portion* of your overall cost is not eligible for the credit. That is, no double-dipping.

A Word For Renters

A closing thought about this matter of double-dipping: note we said above that you can't count expenditures underwritten by Uncle Sam . . . . but didn't say anything about other, *private* parties who might help shoulder the costs.

You're back at the dining room table, Tom and Tammy, gazing out the window wondering how your frostbitten budget will ever withstand another winter like this one.

Let's say you rent your home for $350 a month, and pay the monthly utilities on top as part of the deal. And let's also say that your heating oil bill for last year came to $900.

You recall the local hardware store owner saying that a "modest" investment of $1,000 in caulking and insulation batting for the attic, ought to reduce that fuel bill by at least one-third, or $300—that is to say that the investment would pay for itself in roughly three years. But then again you're renters, and who knows whether you'll be living in the same house three years from now? And so, as you huddle together under a blanket reading this book, it hits you.

You wait until after 2 a.m., when all normal Americans except landlords are sound asleep, and then you call him. Sorry to bother you, you explain, but we have an idea that could save you quite a bit in taxes. Forget the late hour, he is now fully awake.

And then, you clever devils, you offer the following advice: Before New Year's Day (and the end of the tax year), Landlord is to purchase $1,000 worth of the energy-saving supplies discussed above.

He hangs up. You dial back, and push on:

In so doing, you tell him, he, Landlord, will become eligible for a conservation tax credit for 15 percent of the total cost, or $150 right off the top, which will come back to him in the form of an immediate reduction in taxes. He is awed by the command of the tax code that you, a mere renter, display, and is now listening intently. "Yes," he says, "but I am still out $850." (He is, after all, a landlord first and socially conscious citizen second.)

Yes, you say, we know. And although we are mere renters, it would be our pleasure to encourage this socially desirable investment on your part by contributing $250 to help you with the remaining $850 cost. We will contribute this in three equal rent-surcharge payments of $84 each, beginning January 1 of next year.

For the first time in his life, Landlord has heard a renter *ask* for a rent increase. He thinks he is dreaming, or, alternatively, that you have had too much Christmas Cheer. "Why?" he asks softly, not wanting to scare you off.

Here's why, and why it works out to *everyone's* benefit. If the arrangement goes through, Landlord will have acquired $1,000 worth of energy-improvements to his property for $600 ($1,000 cost − $150 tax credit − $250 tenant contribution). He will receive an *immediate* tax reduction of $150 . . . . and additional rental income taxable to him only in the next tax year, leaving him 12 months to figure out how to shelter it from taxation (which, being a landlord, he should have no trouble doing).

You, the renters, will receive an improvement projected to save you $300 in fuel bills next year alone, with *no cash outlay up front*. Over the next three months, it is true, you will have to come up with $250 in extra rent. But those will be *winter* months, likely the heaviest fuel-using months of the year anyway, so you can safely consider those extra rent payments as being offset at least partly by reduced oil bills. Now note: you have committed to paying Landlord $250, but your projected fuel savings in Year 1 will come to $300, so you've saved $50 off the bat. But here's the real kicker: should you continue to rent that house in *Year 2*, your fuel savings will amount *to a full $300*. And that assumes the price of heating oil stays constant, bucking the long-term trend toward ever-spiraling oil prices. For every year you remain in that residence, the $300 savings is yours—and all it "cost" you was a little taxplanning on Landlord's behalf.

And don't forget that there is a third winner in this scenario as well: all of us who want to see our needless national addiction to nonrenewable, air-polluting, foreign-policy-dictating fossil fuels come to an end.

Renewable Energy Source Equipment Tax Credits

This is the second form of federal energy tax credit for the principal residence of a taxpayer, applicable toward the purchase of selected types of *renewable* energy-*producing* equipment.

A couple of introductory words about the renewable energy equipment credit. If you're a renter you can in all likelihood pass this credit by, because it affects equipment-purchases which by their very nature involve major dollar investments. But if you own your own home, here is an opportunity to obtain a huge, fuss-free federal grant toward the energy-improvement of your property, through the backdoor of the tax system.

The credit applies to the purchase of essentially three categories of renewable energy equipment: (1) solar energy systems, of both the "active" and "passive" variety; (2) equipment using geothermal energy; and (3) equipment used to harness wind energy. The credit *is for 40 percent of your total expenditures, up to a credit ceiling of $4,000*; that is, the first $10,000 of expenditures are eligible for the credit, and any costs above that amount are not.

Like the conservation credit described above, the credit is "nonrefundable," meaning that it can't *exceed* the taxes you owe in any particular year so as to leave you with a net gain ("negative income tax") owed you by Uncle Sam. But also like the conservation credit, it can be "carried over:"whatever amount of credit is still left after you've applied it against the taxes owed in the year you bought the equipment, can be carried over to offset the taxes you owe next year, the year after that, and so on, up until the tax year ending Dec. 31, 1987.
Under present law, unless Congress acts otherwise the credit will expire at the end of 1985; expenditures after then will not qualify.

Use of the new equipment must originate with you, Tom Taxpayer—you can't buy a house whose seller installed the equipment and used it, and expect to have his credit passed on to you. But it does appear that you *can* buy a *new* house with such equipment installed by the builder—or an old house with such equipment that's just been installed, and never used—and take the credit.* The rule applicable to the conservation credit, that construction of the principal residence must have been substantially completed by April 20, 1977, does *not* apply in the case of the equipment credit.

Several final rules. First, the equipment you buy must reasonably be expected to remain in operation for at least five years. It must also meet quality standards set forth in any regulatory standards applicable to the property. (Neither of these rules should scare you off, for they're both designed to protect your consumer interests.) Second, the equipment credit, like its conservation brother, is a one-shot deal as far as your residence is concerned. You can obtain up to $4,000 in equipment credits for a personal residence and *that's it* for the life of that residence as long as you're the owner (although, of course, when you move to another home you become eligible all over again to take credits for the energy improvements you make on it). Third, no "double-dipping"— you can't claim the credit for any portion of the cost financed by a government subsidy or non-taxable grant.

The Adjustment To Basis Rule

The fourth and final rule is somewhat tricky. Suppose you bought your home for $50,000. Suppose, also, that in five years you sell it for $100,000. Assuming that no real-estate tax-sheltering devices apply (see Chapter 4) you will owe tax on the $50,000 "profit" you realize upon the sale of the property. Now suppose, instead, that while you lived in the house you added a new room, at a cost of $20,000. Suddenly that $100,000 sale is not netting you a $50,000 "prof-

---

* Take one builder in the suburbs of Denver whose single-family detached homes offer a solar-powered hot-water system also expected to heat a portion of the main living area. The system is designed to save owners around 80 percent of their home-hot water bills and 25 percent of their space heating costs. The system costs $5,500, and the builder passes on the federal credit he's entitled to—$2,200—to the homebuyer. With the units costing between $85,500—89,500 each, a buyer could find about half of his five percent downpayment requirement underwritten indirectly by Uncle Sam!

it," but only $30,000, and it would be unfair to ask you to pay tax on anything more than $30,000. The federal tax laws recognize this by a device known as "adjusting the basis" of your property. At the time you bought your house, its price, $50,000, also became its "basis," to use taxtalk. And at the time you added the room, its $20,000 price-tag was tacked on to the basis: the basis of your home was "adjusted upward" to $70,000. And upon sale, the sales price is reduced by the adjusted basis to come up with the $30,000 profit figure.

Now the example gets a bit more complicated when, instead of using a $20,000 room-addition as the improvement, we use, say, a $20,000 installation of an active solar space-heating system instead. The adjusted basis would still *appear* to be $70,000 —but that would *not* take into account the federal tax credit of $4,000 (40 percent × $10,000 maximum credit-eligible expenditure) you took at the time you installed the equipment. So, the $70,000 adjusted basis of your home must be further adjusted *downward* by the amount of the credit ($4,000) to $66,000, to prevent you from reaping a veritable windfall at Uncle Sam's expense.

Why It's Still Worth The Effort

Now this may leave you thinking, aha! I'm *losing* my credit . . . . it's not worth the effort . . . . what a fraud! That is, it may leave you thinking that all this tax shelter allowed you to do was to *defer* paying taxes between the time you took the credit and the time you sold your house. But that's not so! And why it's not so depends once again on the critical difference between a *credit* and a *deduction*, and between *ordinary* income and *capital gains* income.

Think back to the credit you took: it was for $4,000, applied *directly* against *the taxes you owed*. You *saved* $4,000, *period*. Now when you sell your house, for an after-credit "profit" of $34,000, two things happen.

First, that entire $4,000 of extra "profit" is not taxed away *in entirety*. It's taxed *only to the extent of your marginal* tax rate. Second, the "profits" you've made are not taxed as ordinary income but as capital gains; that is, at 40 percent of your ordinary-income tax bracket. Assuming you're in the 35 percent bracket, this means that you will be paying only .4 × .35 × $4,000 = $560 of that $4,000 credit back to Uncle Sam in taxes! That's a bare 14 percent of the credit! So you see, the renewable source credit, *despite* the downward basis-adjustment requirement, is *not* merely a deferral-type tax shelter . . . . it is also a conversion-type shelter *and* an outright, forever savings shelter of great power if you know how to use it. Let's turn to that.

How To Use The Equipment Credit

Let's say you own a typical 25 year-old home, with typical spouse and two typical children. Your annual hot water bill comes to $1,200 (for heating water electrically). You are 35 years old, have seen the sun rise and set every day of your life and have no reason to expect the cycle to stop any time soon; in short, you suspect that solar energy may be a viable option for hot-water heating in your home.

You invite three reputable solar-equipment retailers over to examine the premises and make their recommendations, and they all go something like this: for around $3,500, we can install a solar hot-water system that will net you an average annual savings of 80 percent of your electricity bill attributable to hot-water costs.

You shake your head in disgust, silently acknowledging the Seven Sister oil giants' stranglehold on our economy: how shall I come up with $3,500, you ask the bathroom mirror? And besides—even at these most optimistic of predictions—it will take *almost four years* [$3,500 cost ÷ (80 percent × $1,200) =3.6 years] to make back my original investment in solar energy. Maybe Zonker is right, and the sun is best left to tanning purposes.

Think again, Tom. Suppose, just suppose, that you can make that $3,500 purchase with a 10 percent downpayment, and a loan for the remaining $3,150 at 12 percent for five years. Using the same fuel-saving figures and assuming you're in the 40 percent marginal tax bracket, here's what happens over each of those five years:

Year	Cash Outlay	Tax Savings	Loan Costs	Fuel Savings	Net Gain	Cumulative Gain
I	$350	$1,400	-0-	$960	$2,010	$2,010
II	-0-	$151	$1008	$960	$103	$2113
III	-0-	$121	$932	$960	$139	$2,262
IV	-0-	$91	$857	$960	$194	$2,456
V	-0-	$60	$781	$960	$239	$2,695
VI	-0-	$30	$706	$960	$284	$2,979

What happens is simply this: thanks to the magic of two aspects of the tax system—the renewable energy source equipment tax credit, and the deductibility of the interest on your loan—you actually come out *ahead* in *each* of the first five years you own the system and are paying off your loan. In fact, taking into account the 40 percent credit (which is not adversely affected by the fact that your downpayment is only 10 percent of the purchase price), you come out ahead *more than $2,000* the year you buy the system, and almost $3,000 ahead by the time the loan is paid in full. And once the system is paid for, of course, that $960 fuel savings is yours free-and-clear forever—that is, until you sell your house, at which time you can expect at least a portion of the solar hot water system's market value to be reflected in the sales price. *You win*, anyway you slice it.

If you believe we need to start conserving our scarce energy resources . . . . or that the sun, the wind, and the heat trapped beneath the earth's surface are potentially cost-effective, commercially sensible methods of providing ourselves with safe, clean, reliable domestically produced energy . . . . *invest* in that belief—*to your profit*—with Uncle Sam right at your side.

6

Tax Exempt Bonds: How Uncle Sam Can Help You Fund A Favorite Public Project

One need only tune in the nightly news to hear almost daily reports on the devastating impact Reaganomics has had on the cities. A recent study by the U.S. Conference of Mayors finds that consolidation of what were formerly 56 federal urban programs into nine block grants to the states, has caused cuts in employment and training, health services and emergency care for the elderly and other needy groups, ranging 50 percent and higher in some instances. The American city, where most Americans spend most of their lives, is hurting and hurting bad. In the meantime, the defense establishment is getting a five-year, *$1.6 trillion* shot in the arm.

Wouldn't it be nice, instead, for *you* to be able to re-direct our tax dollars into the kinds of state, county and local public services you feel Uncle Sam ought to help provide? Well, you can—and can save some extra bucks in the bargain.

The mechanism for doing so is the tax-exempt bond. It goes under quite a few names—the "muni" (for municipal), industrial revenue bond, general obligation bond, etc.—to reflect all the variations the market can provide. But the central theme is the same. The instrument we are interested in is a "bond"—a form of commercial contract between you, as lender, and the bond-issuer, as borrower, to pay you a specified sum of money at some specified future date. Between the day you buy the bond, and the date it "matures" (you get your loan back) or else the day you sell it on the bond market, you will collect a specified rate of interest. And in the case of tax-exempt bonds, that interest is *always* exempt from federal income tax, and often exempt from state tax as well. Simple enough.

So you grab your local newspaper. Turning to the financial page, your eyes race across the bond market listings looking for the "tax exempts." Bam! You make a horrible discovery: the interest rates offered on tax-exempt bonds are consistently *below* the rates offered on non-tax exempts! So why buy them?

Why Do Tax-Exempt Bonds Exist?

The reason is, Tom and Tammy, that for nearly 150 years the Congress and the courts have gone out of their way to try to make it easier for governments to raise money than for profit-making (or profit-attempting) companies. The logic is that each and every American benefits from making the fiercely competitive money markets somewhat more accessible to borrowers who will use the cash to pay for public projects like hospitals, sewage-treatment plants and the like. By allowing the interest paid on such bonds to be tax-exempt, Congress has in effect enabled the issuers to pay a lower rate and still stay competitive, saving literally billions of dollars thereby.

But wait a minute. A tax exemption is a privilege which allows you, the taxpayer, to exclude a sum of income from your taxable income, *not* from the taxes you actually owe. In this respect it acts quite a bit like a tax deduction (and *not* like a credit), in the sense that how much a particular exemption is worth to *you*, depends upon how much *you* otherwise earn, and what tax bracket that puts *you* in. In other words, not only is the tax-exempt bond system good for cities; it's gr-e-e-e-a-a-t, as Tony the Tiger would say, for the truly well-to-do.

How Much Is Tax-Free Interest Worth To You?

That's true. But you will be surprised to learn, just the same, *how little* you have to earn to make tax-exempt bond-buying worth your while. In fact, in today's interest-rate climate, it becomes reasonable for you to consider tax-exempt

bonds as a good "tax shelter" if you find yourself in a 30
percent marginal tax bracket or higher. Under current tax
rates, the 30 percent bracket is reached when taxable income
(on a joint return) exceeds $30,000. According to the Dean
Witter Reynolds, Inc. securities firm, "For most couples who
have normal deductions and a total of, say, four exemptions,
this will occur when gross annual income is in the $36-40,000
range. For single taxpayers, the break-point begins in the
mid-20's."

The table on the following page, also composed by Dean
Witter Reynolds, Inc., shows how you can "translate" the
value of a tax-exempt bond interest rate into a non-exempt
interest rate for your own income bracket. The row across
the top shows various taxable incomes (in thousands of
dollars) for taxpayers filing single returns, and the row immediately under it is for joint returns. The third row tells
you what marginal tax bracket that amount of taxable income would put you in. (For instance, if you file a single
return and your taxable income is $25,000, you fall into the
30 percent marginal tax bracket, meaning that of each *additional* dollar of ordinary income (up to a total income of
$28,800), 30 cents would be taken away in federal income
taxes.) The far-left column of numbers represent various
hypothetical interest rates paid on tax-exempt bonds. Each
successive column tells you the interest rate that a non-tax-
exempt bond would have to pay to yield the *same* after-tax
return to a person in any particular tax bracket.

So let's say you're in the 30 percent bracket, as before.
A tax exempt bond yielding 7 percent would be "worth" the
same to you, *all else being equal,* as a non-tax-exempt yielding
10 percent. A 12 percent-yielding tax-exempt would be worth
as a non-tax-exempt yielding 17.1 percent, and so on.

This table reflects rates in effect for taxable years beginning after 1983. Thus the benefit for short-term investments,
made in the interim period of higher tax rates, will be
understated.

HOW MUCH IS TAX-FREE INTEREST INCOME WORTH TO YOU?

Taxable Income

TAX-EXEMPT RATES	26%	28%	30%	33%	34%	38%	42%	45%	48%	49%	50%
Single Return	$18,200–23,500		$23,500–28,800		$28,800–34,100		$34,100–41,500	$41,500–55,300	$55,300–81,800		81,800+
Joint Return		$29,900–35,200		$35,200–45,800		$45,800–60,000	$60,000–85,600	$85,600–109,400		$109,400–162,400	$162,400+
Tax Bracket	26%	28%	30%	33%	34%	38%	42%	45%	48%	49%	50%
NON-EXEMPT EQUIVALENT											
7	9.5	9.7	10.0	10.4	10.6	11.3	12.1	12.7	13.5	13.7	14.0
8	10.8	11.1	11.4	11.9	12.1	12.9	13.8	14.5	15.4	15.7	16.0
9	12.2	12.5	12.9	13.4	13.6	14.5	15.5	16.4	17.3	17.6	18.0
10	13.5	13.9	14.3	14.9	15.2	16.1	17.2	18.2	19.2	19.6	20.0
11	14.9	15.3	15.7	16.4	16.7	17.7	19.0	20.0	21.2	21.6	22.0
12	16.2	16.7	17.1	17.9	18.2	19.4	20.7	21.8	23.1	23.5	24.0
13	17.6	18.1	18.6	19.4	19.7	21.0	22.4	23.6	25.0	25.5	26.0
14	18.9	19.4	20.0	20.9	21.2	22.6	24.1	25.5	26.9	27.5	28.0

Source: Abridged from "Tax Free Muni Bonds—The Direct Path to Lower Federal Income Taxes," Dean Witter Reynolds, Inc.

Marketability And Security

What do we mean, "all else being equal?" We mean that there are other factors besides a raw rate-of-return figure that one looks for when buying a bond. Chief among them are "marketability" and "security." It's unlikely, for instance, you'd want to buy a bond yielding 25 percent if you knew at the time of purchase that only Incan descendants residing in Norway would be interested in buying it from you—that's much too "illiquid" an investment for most of us. Similarly, you'd probably not be inclined to purchase a 25 percent yielding bond issued by Rock Bottom Railroad, knowing that bankruptcy for the company was probable within the month.

As you might expect, the higher the marketability and security of a particular bond issue, the lower its "yield" (the amount of interest it pays, expressed as a fraction of the bond's price.)

Going back to our table to find an example, note again that a taxpayer in the 34 percent marginal tax bracket buying a tax-exempt bond yielding 12 percent will net the same after-tax income as from a non-tax exempt yielding 18.2 percent; but *to find* a non-tax-exempt bond yielding 18.2 percent may mean setting one's sights quite a bit lower on marketability and security. Hence, tax-exempts can offer the alert investor a particularly attractive package of yield, marketability, and security. And for the alert, Progressive-minded investor, there is the added bonus of knowing with great specificity to what public purpose particular bond revenues will be put.

To be sure, tax-exempt municipal bonds have their risks too. Like their non-exempt corporate counterparts, the moneys they raise can be put to uses as different as night and day—some far more secure, some more socially sensible.

General Obligation And Revenue Bonds

Tax-exempt bonds generally fall into one of two categories. First, there are "general obligation" bonds, the sort that may be issued by a municipality to cover general operating costs. General obligation bonds are backed by the "full faith and credit" of the issuing authority, including its general taxing powers. They are generally considered quite safe (although their relative safety will of course vary with the overall fiscal health of the issuer). The second general category is the "revenue bond." Revenue bonds are most often tied to a particular public-works project (or, in the case of mortgage-revenue or industrial-revenue bonds, to the particular purpose identified therein). These bonds are usually secured by the projected revenues of the enterprise they underwrite. This may mean toll-road receipts in the case of a highway; tuition fees from a publicly supported educational institution; lease rental income, payments for electricity, and so on. In the case of revenue bonds, unlike general obligation bonds, you can identify quite specifically the particular project or purpose to which the bond-funds will be put. And that fact gives you, the buyer, a considerable amount of sway in determining what sorts of public projects *you* want *your* tax dollars to finance.

A good, very recent real-life example involves one form of revenue bond steadily gaining in popularity, the so-called "pollution control" bond. These bonds are a Congressionally-sanctioned financing device through which a public entity with the authority to issue tax-exempt bonds, raises the money to construct pollution control facilities for power-plants owned by a second entity (usually a private, for-profit utility or a rural electric cooperative).

In October of 1982, two of the many such pollution-control bond offerings to hit the market were (1) a $70 million offering by the Lehigh County, Pa. Industrial Development Authority, and (2) a $60 million offering by the Deseret Generation and Transmission Co-operative Project of Uintah County, Utah. Both offerings involved efforts to raise capital to install pollution control facilities on power plants under construction. Both were tax-exempt to the buyer. Both offered yields upon issue in the 10-11 percent range. But for the socially conscious investor-taxpayer, there was one big difference. The Deseret plant is a coal-fired generating unit. The Lehigh facility is nuclear-fueled.

The point of the above is merely to illustrate that within just one narrow class of tax-exempts—pollution control—lies a broad range of highly controversial public pursuits which you can elect either to support or reject *with Uncle Sam's support*. Around the country, tax-exempt industrial- revenue bonds (IDB's) are being used to help finance new commercial enterprises, many in particularly depressed areas. By some estimates, as much as $8 billion in IDB's were sold in 1982 to subsidize lower-rate mortgages for housing, much of it for low-income tenants. Other tax-exempt bond revenues are enabling rural communities to offer interest-subsidized loans to farmers for needed improvements and expansion. In its lame-duck moments, the Congress in 1982 gave Indian tribal governments the authority to issue certain kinds of tax-exempts to finance their public needs too. The list goes on and on—the point is, you are bound to find tax-exempt investment options that are substantially equal in respect to yield, security, and marketability . . . . but *not* in their ultimate social objective.

How About A Swap?

Now you're getting mad . . . . real mad. "The point of this book was to show me how to save taxes, not how to make 'socially aware' investments with money I don't have," you interject. Well, hold on a minute. Do you, Tom, or you, Tammy, own *any* securities (stocks or bonds) at the present time? And if so, are they worth less than what you paid for them? Then a "swap" may be for you.

Let's suppose you own 100 shares of XYZ stock, which you bought four years ago at $20 a share. XYZ is currently trading around $11 a share, a fact which convinces you (a) you'll never invest in the stock market again; and (b) you'd be a fool to sell now and lose $900 of your original investment. You haven't been back to the barber who gave you that "hot tip" since.

Perusing the bond listings in your morning paper (which you do because they face the comics and you're too tired to turn the page), you come across a tax-exempt bond originally issued to finance low-rate mortages to low and moderate income would-be homebuyers. Its "coupon yield" (the interest rate as a fraction of its $100 issue price) was 8 percent. However, because interest rates generally are considerably higher today, market forces have pushed the bond's *price* downward in order to bring its *current yield* into line with others of similar marketability and security. Hence, the bond is listed at $90—it is what is known in the trade as a "discount bond" because its yield to "maturity" (the date on which the original contract of $100 will be paid) is more than the coupon yield. This particular bond matures in 1993, ten years from now. Hence, its actual yield is as follows:

(1) Original yield = 8 percent of $100 issue price = $8, Current price = $90. $90 ÷ $8 = 8.9 percent actual "market yield." Figuring you are in a 30 percent marginal tax bracket, an 8.9 percent tax-exempt yield translates into roughly a 12.7 percent after-tax return. PLUS:

(2) The $90 bond will be redeemed for $100 in ten years. Therefore, its value will increase by $10 (11 percent of its purchase price) over 10 years = 1.1 percent a year averaged out.

Your total yield on the bond, assuming you hold it till maturity, will be about 13.8 percent a year. Of course, should interest rates generally suddenly drop, your bond would become more attractive to prospective purchasers (because of its fixed interest rate) and its value would rise, allowing you to sell in advance of maturity for a profit (which would be taxed, but at the lower capital gains rate).

All in all, you decide that your prospects of making money are at least as good if you buy the bond, as if you hold onto your shares in XYZ. From your point of view, *today*, the investments are of equal value to you.

That being the case, Uncle Sam would like to encourage you to make the "swap." Why? Who knows—and who cares. The point is, if you sell your shares in XYZ corporation, your

$900 loss will generate an important tax benefit in the form of a capital loss deduction (the opposite of capital gains income). Because you've owned the stock more than a year, you have what is called a $900 long-term capital loss. The special tax rule for long-term capital losses is this: every dollar of loss offsets *50 cents* of *ordinary income*, up to a limit of $3,000 a year. Any excess over $3,000 may be carried over, i.e. to offset up to $3,000 of ordinary income (50 cents to the dollar) in future years, until the entire amount of the loss is used up. Your loss is $900; hence you can subtract $450 from the income you will be taxed on this year. And because you're in the 30 percent marginal tax bracket, your actual tax savings will be about .3 $\times$ $450 = $135. Had you owned your stock less than a year, the $900 would be classified as a short-term capital loss, which could then offset ordinary income dollar-for-dollar (instead of only 50 cents to the dollar), again, up to $3,000 a year.

Note what you've been able to accomplish. First of all, you've transferred your assets, out of a financially unproductive investment into a financially *and socially* more productive one. Second, Uncle Sam has rewarded you for your astuteness by giving you $150 back on your federal income taxes.

This kind of "swap" works fine from any form of stock or bond into another, provided you play by the rules. Don't, for instance, think you can get away with declaring a loss by selling your XYZ stock and then simply buying it right back again; the swap routine won't work if the investments are "substantially identical" and both transactions occur within 30 days of each other. And to be completely safe, always check out the tax ramifications of a swap with your broker (and tax advisor if you have one) before you make the transaction.

7

Charitable Donations—The Gift Uncle Sam Keeps On Giving

Anticipate charity by preventing poverty; assist the reduced fellowman, either by a considerable gift, or a sum of money, or by teaching him a trade, or by putting him in the way of business so that he may earn an honest livelihood, and not be forced to the dreadful alternative of holding out his hand for charity. This is the highest step and the summit of charity's golden ladder.

Maimonides, 12th century

When the rich assemble to concern themselves with the business of the poor it is called charity. When the poor assemble to concern themselves with the business of the rich it is called anarchy.

Paul Richard, 1929.

Those of you savvy taxplanners who *really* know your history will appreciate that it was the Salvation Army, responsible more than anyone or anything else, for getting Christmas on the calendar at December's end. And do you *really* think Thanksgiving falls late in the year just because some colonists had a bountiful corn harvest back in 1621? Nonsense! Now, if the Internal Revenue Service could *really* have its way, these occasions when "giving" is most on the national mind would quietly be relocated to a time of year when taxes are not. It would kick the crutches out from under Tiny Tim and confiscate Christmas Seals as contraband.

Why? Because each year, millions of American taxpayers give billions in gifts to qualified charities, and the amounts they give always go up as the end of the tax year gets closer.

"Charitable giving? C'mon! What do *we*, Tom and Tammy Taxpayer, scraping as never before just to pay our own bills, possibly have in common with the Rockefellers and the Vanderbilts? Charitable projects are the privileged domain of the rich," you stammer.

Some Reasons To Consider Charitable Gifts

Now hold on. Before we even get into the art of charitable gift-giving—and it *is* an art—here are three good financial reasons why *you* ought to keep reading:

• Charitable giving is one of the few tax-saving devices you can use effectively *right up to the end of the tax year.* If everything we've said about the wisdom of tax-planning starting January 1 has passed you by, *this* "tax shelter" may still help you out *this* year.

• You probably have a heck of alot of charitable contributions to deduct *already*, and don't know it—or don't know how to take advantage of it.

• Recent changes in the tax laws may have made it easier than ever for you to reduce your tax bill this way. Starting with the 1982 tax year, taxpayers who don't itemize their deductions, but take the standard deduction or use the "short form," will be able to take charitable deductions just the same. (This provision is due to expire at the end of 1986, but applies to tax years 1982-86.)

And a fourth, more socially oriented reason, as put by a coalition of community-based foundations called the Funding Exchange:

> "One may find it contradictory to be concerned about a more equitable distribution of wealth in society and to be taking advantage of tax breaks available primarily to those with high and/or unearned incomes . . . . (O)ur response is that it seems to be a much greater contradiction *not* to avoid taxes considering where the federal tax dollar presently goes and the fact that the government itself encourages you by law to take full advantage of every available tax benefit. It wouldn't make sense to have most people doing everything they can to reduce their taxes, while more socially responsible people neglect tax deductions and see a higher percentage of their

annual income go for financing the latest Pentagon missile system."*

The ways in which tax-advantaged charitable gifts may be made are many—so many, in fact, that the field is a highly specialized one with accountants, attorneys and other full-time professionals unto its own. In this chapter we can only summarize some of the more popular ways that charitable gift-giving can work for *you*—the moderate—income tax-payer in search of shelter from shameless federal spending. To ram home the point that you don't have to be a Rockefeller to reap the goodies of giving, we'll approach the subject *not* from the point of view of who you give to, or how much you give, but *how* you give.

The "Ultra-Tiny" Donation

So you don't envision yourself a philanthropist? Just the same, you didn't *really* turn a cold shoulder last Halloween when those adorable goblins showed up on your doorstep with their UNICEF boxes, now did you? Even Scrooge drops *something* in the Salvation Army pot each Christmas.

Did you drive your car to and from a volunteer activity, paying for the gas, oil and so on yourself? Give a membership fee to your church? Attend a benefit concert? Give old clothes away to a community fund? Take part in your employer's United Way Campaign?

Nobody isn't on *somebody's* fundraising mailing list anymore. The point is, whether you remember it or not, whether you *record* it or not, you'd be a highly unusual American if you didn't give *some* amount away to "qualified charitable organizations" during the year. (We'll come soon to who and what actually does qualify.) But you would be absolutely typical not to keep accurate records of these "ultra-tiny" donations; it hardly seems worth the effort.

Gift Giving Guide—Methods and Tax Implications of Giving Away Money, by the Funding Exchange (135 East 15th Street, New York, NY 10013), New York, 1981, Pp. ix-x.)

Let's say these ultra-tinys aggregate up to $100 in a particular year. What that's worth to you in taxes saved, depends on: (a) your tax bracket, and (b) whether you itemize your tax deductions, or take what is called the "standard deduction" instead of itemizing. We'll assume you're married, filing a joint return, and your taxable income for the 1983 tax year is $30,000, which puts you in the 30 percent marginal tax bracket (meaning that 30 cents of your *next* dollar of income above $30,000, would depart you in taxes).

Your decision whether or not to itemize will depend completely on which amount is greater: the standard deduction for a person of your tax status, or the sum of your itemized deductions.

The standard deduction for tax year 1983 is as follows:

For	Amount of the Deduction
single taxpayers	$2300
married, filing a joint return	3400
head of household	2300
married, filing separately	1700

To find out whether or not your itemized deductions for the same year exceed the amount in your category, you need to take a look at the Schedules A & B section of the Form 1040 tax return, which is what you use to derive your actual taxable income from your adjusted gross income. In practice, to make itemizing worth your while you will have to have substantial deductions in one or more of four main categories: medical bills or losses from theft or casualty; state and local tax payments (including property taxes); loan and/or mortgage interest payments, or—you guessed it—charitable contributions.

Let's assume the sum of your itemized deductions is $4,000, and you itemize. Your $100 in charitable contributions is deductible and, because you're in the 30 percent bracket, your actual tax savings will approach $30.

Note what that means, Tom and Tammy. By keeping careful track of *what* you give away, Uncle Sam will allow you *either* to get one-third of it back, *or* to increase your total giving by about one-third without spending any more of your own money. Now consider that the sum of "ultra-tiny" giving nationwide every year probably ranges well beyond the billion-dollar mark, and you'll get some idea of why it might be wise to start keeping track.

"Ultra-Tiny" Tracking For Non-Itemizers

In 1981, for the first time, Congress made it worth your while to keep track of "ultra-tiny" giving even if you *don't* itemize. Marginally worth your while, but worth it nonetheless.

Since enactment of the Reagan tax program the newspapers have run full of accounts predicting hard times for charities of all kinds. The basis for those predictions is the fact that under the Reagan plan personal income brackets have been falling dramatically and will continue doing so—especially the top income brackets—making charitable giving steadily less "attractive" to the upper-bracket donor. The table on the following page, prepared by the Funding Exchange, illustrates just how the tax "value" of a $100 deductible charitable gift would decrease for donors of varying income levels from 1981-84.

It's all true—yet there is a counterbalancing factor still to be taken into account. And that's the fact that in 1981, for the first time, Congress made it possible for donors who *don't* itemize their tax deductions to get *some* tax advantage from gifts anyway. Here's how that works:

Beginning in tax year 1982, non-itemizers could treat 25 percent of their contributions—up to a ceiling of $100—as deductible. In other words, if you gave $100 that year, your deduction was for 25 percent of $100 = $25. (Your actual tax savings, though, was only your deduction times your tax bracket, or $25 × 33 percent = $8.25.) The same limits hold true for tax year 1983. For tax year 1984, the 25 percent-of-contribution limit still holds the same, but the ceiling on contributions will rise from $100 to $300. In 1985, the contribu-

The tax savings produced by making a charitable gift of $100:			
Taxable Income:	Single	Head of Household	Married
—1981—*			
$10,000	$21	$22	$18
20,000	34	31	24
30,000	44	42	37
40,000	49	46	43
50,000	55	54	49
100,000	68	63	59
—1982—			
$10,000	$19	$20	$16
20,000	31	28	22
30,000	40	38	33
40,000	44	41	39
50,000	50	48	44
100,000	50	50	50
—1983—			
$10,000	$17	$18	$15
20,000	28	25	19
30,000	36	34	30
40,000	40	37	35
50,000	45	44	40
100,000	50	50	48
—1984—			
$10,000	$16	$17	$14
20,000	26	24	18
30,000	34	32	28
40,000	38	35	33
50,000	42	42	38
100,000	50	50	45

Source: *Gift Giving Guide*, P.4.

* The 1.25% tax credit for 1981 federal income taxes is not reflected in this chart. Its impact on any tax savings due to tax deductions was negligible.

tion ceiling is eliminated entirely, and the percentage limitation rises to 50 percent. And in 1986, your contribution becomes fully deductible and their is no ceiling—in other words, the non-itemizer and the itemizer are treated as equals for charitable-gift purposes. In 1987, the provision for non-itemizer giving deductions expires. Oh well.

The point of this exercise is to show that the tax laws on charitable giving are likely to affect *you*, Tom and Tammy, even if your giving is limited to the "ultra-tinys"—that is, where the tax implications are really little more than an afterthought, and not a driving force behind your donation. It behooves you to make an effort this year to set aside a section in your financial records called "Charitable Contributions." Then, *each time* you make a gift—even if only for $1.00—make a proper notation as to date, recipient, and form of payment (cash, check, in-kind gift such as old clothing, etc.). Whenever possible, obtain "substantiation" for your donation (a receipt will do fine). Clip those receipts to this section of your records; you'll probably be amazed how substantially those ultra-tinys will add up come tax time.

Increasing Your Tiny-Gift Tax Break

Now let's elevate the stakes a notch: what can you do to *increase* your tax-take from such small charitable giving? For one thing, start your spring cleaning *before* spring arrives. Dig out all the old clothes, discarded furniture, an old TV set, some dusty books—the stuff of which goodwill donations are made—and arrange for them to be delivered to and accepted by an appropriate receiving organization. The value of your deduction (subject to the itemize/non-itemize distinction noted above) is the "fair market value" of the merchandise you give away—normally what a willing buyer would be willing to pay a willing seller in the open marketplace. (To get a sense of what that is, one gentleman I know phones classified ads offering merchandise like that he wants to donate, haggles over prices until he and the would-be seller "strike a bargain," and then hangs up.)

Donating with Determination

You're believers, strong believers, in the importance of conserving our natural resources, and you want to give more than token financial support to that particular cause. While not exactly capable of patron-saint-size philanthropy, you place yourself in that category of taxpayer who can afford to put one to five percent of your income aside for this and other charitable purposes. How do the tax laws help you?

Substantially—if you itemize. And amazingly, if you use a little ingenuity in your giving style.

Let's take the simplest example first. Say, you've set aside three percent of your $27,000 gross income—$800—for charitable pursuits in tax year 1983. What can and can't you do?

First, overcome the startlingly common misconception that the tax laws impose limits on the amount of charitable contributions you can *make* in any particular year. They do absolutely no such thing—but the tax laws *do* set important limits on the amount of contributions that you can *deduct* in any particular year, and that amount is tied, not surprisingly, to the amount of your taxable income. Here's how it works.

Identifying Charitable Groups

The first key step is to identify the tax-character of the organization you wish to support. Note the deliberate use of the term "organization;" individuals, no matter how needy, cannot be "charities" eligible to receive tax-deductible contributions. Nor are all not-for-profit organizations which are *themselves* exempt from having to pay income taxes ("tax exempt"), necessarily groups contributions to which are tax-deductible to *you*. It's a bit more complicated than that.

In order to receive your contribution and have it serve as a tax deduction for you, a philanthropic organization must be organized and operated exclusively for a *public* purpose that is religious, charitable, scientific, literary, educational, designed to foster national or international amateur sports competition (other than provision of athletic facilities or equipment), or aimed at preventing cruelty to children or animals. (Alternatively, the recipient organization may be the United States Government or any of its "political subdivisions" such as a state, county or city. More about this in Chapter 13.)

Many—but certainly not all—of these organizations are included under a particular section of the Internal Revenue Code, Sec. 501(c)(3), as nonprofit, tax-exempt public charities. When considering making a contribution, ask the organization to produce its 501(c)(3) certification letter from the IRS; if it has the designation this shouldn't be a problem. Alternatively, you can check with your local IRS office to see if the group is so listed.

There are other organizations, however, whose "organizational purpose" fits the bill with no problems, but which have not been officially recognized by the IRS. To guide you in determining whether the group you're interested in giving to, would qualify for 501(c)(3) status, check the list below to see if its "organizational purpose" fits within any of the specific categories which IRS itself uses in determining charitable activity:

• Relief of the poor and distressed or of the underprivileged
• Advancement of religion
• Advancement of education or science
• Erection or maintenance of public buildings, monuments or works
• Lessening of the burdens of government
• Promotion of social welfare by organizations designed to accomplish any of the above purposes, or:
—to lessen neighborhood tensions;
—to eliminate prejudice or discrimination;
—to defend human and civil rights secured by law;

—to combat community deterioration and juvenile delinquency.*

There are also certain purposes which the IRS considers *not* to be charitable. Of course, if the group operates primarily to make a profit, that won't do. If its purpose is to spread "propaganda," as opposed to a "full and fair representation" of a particular issue, that is considered a noncharitable activity. If it lobbies government officials using either: (a) more than an "insubstantial" amount of its overall financial resources, or (b) more than a specified percentage of its funds (which percentage you should be able to obtain from the group's accounting staff), it will not qualify, *and* may be in danger of losing its Sec. 501(c)(3) status if it's already obtained it. And finally, if the group benefits only a closed, limited circle of people—like a trade association—it is apt not to qualify.**

Public Charity Or Private Foundation

So we've determined that the object of your charitable charms is a qualified charitable organization. The next step is to determine into which of two broad categories it falls: the *public charity*, or the *private foundation*. In either case, your contribution will be "tax advantaged"—that is, you will be eligible for *some* deduction. But if your donation is substantial, *how much* that deduction is ultimately worth will depend on which category your group falls into.

* Taken from *The Gift Giving Guide*, P. 16.)

** Before we move on, you should know that there sometimes *is* a way to support a non-tax-exempt, non 501(c)(3) group and *still* get your deduction. The secret is that qualified charities, like those involved in grant-making activities, *may* make *their own* grants to non-qualifying groups, provided the money so given is restricted exclusively for use toward a qualified charitable purpose. So if you can find a qualified charity which will assume the role of "fiscal sponsor," *it* can accept your (tax-deductible) contribution and then make an equal-sized grant to the non-exempt group of your choice. Just another case, Tom and Tammy, of a tax loophole loosening up for those who know the ropes.

Charitable Donations   91

Private foundations first. They are classified under Sec. 509(a) of the Internal Revenue Code, so if the group you wish to give to tells you it's a Section 509(a) organization, then you know you're dealing with a private foundation. But in all likelihood, it will be up to you to determine for yourself whether the group is one or the other. The key to which is which is, essentially, the *breadth of the sources of funding* for the organization. Suppose a close friend has died; a charity is being created in his honor. The goal is to raise $20,000 over a five-year period, with four relatives and close friends, you being one, pledged to $1,000 a year each. The question for tax purposes is: is this organization "publicly supported?" In *most* cases, a handy rule-of-thumb developed by charitable giving experts is that if more than 17 donors are involved, the IRS will tend to find that the entity is "publicly supported." In this instance, that is evidently not the case. It looks like you're dealing, therefore, with a private foundation.

The 20 Percent Rule For Private Foundations

The significance of the distinction from your point of view, Tom and Tammy Taxpayer, is as follows: a contribution to a "private foundation" is eligible for a charitable deduction in the year of donation, up to a ceiling of *20 percent* of your adjusted gross income in that year. If your adjusted gross income for 1983 is $20,000, then your maximum charitable deduction for the year is 20 percent × $20,000 = $4,000. No problem in the example posed above. *But* had you given the above-described foundation $5,000 *in a single year*, $1,000 worth of tax deduction would have been lost *forever*.

The 50 Percent Carryover Rule For Public Charities

In the case of a "public charity," there are two crucial distinctions. The first is the percentage limitation: you can deduct donations to public charities up to *50 percent* of your adjusted gross income in the year of donation. In the example just used, $10,000 would be your charitable-deduction ceiling. The second crucial distinction is that when giving to public charities any *excess over* the 50 percent limit, you can *carry over* that excess to the following five tax years. Unless you're Mother Teresa, it's highly unlikely that you'll be giving away one-half your adjusted gross income a year. But in the event you do, it's nice to know that the full amount of your contribution will ultimately be deductible by applying the excess to tax year 1984, then tax year 1985, and so on until the surplus is exhausted.

Contributions of Appreciated Property

There is an important exception to this 50 percent rule, but it applies to something we haven't discussed yet: the contribution of property *other than cash*. This topic is so potentially important to you that we're going to give it alot of attention all its own. Follow along closely.

Let's suppose that three years ago, you bought 100 shares of stock in a fly-by-night pornographic movie distributor, Fly By Night Productions, Inc., for $2.00 per share. The company expanded into children's feature-films, lucking out one year with a charming supernatural kiddie flick, *D.T.*, and its price-per-share flew by day to $20. Your marginal tax rate is 45 percent, let's assume.

What that stock represents to you is *substantially appreciated property*. If you were to sell it at $20 per share, you would be liable for *long-term capital gains* tax on your profits (long-term because you owned it for more than one year). Only 40 percent of long-term capital gains are subject to federal income tax; hence, you would owe .4 × ($20-2) × 100 shares × 45 percent bracket = $324 in taxes on your profit of $1800.

Now here comes a bit of tax magic. Suppose that, instead of actually selling the stock, you *donate* it to a properly recognized charity. Look carefully at what happens:

First—because you have held the property over one year and would recognize long-term capital gains, the tax code allows you to take a charitable deduction for the *full fair market value* ($20 per share) of the stock.

Second—because you're donating away your shares instead of cashing them in, you *never* have to pay any tax on the difference between the purchase price and sales price, your *profit*.

In other words, Tom and Tammy, by donating appreciated long-term capital gains property, you save taxes—*twice*. And how much you actually save depends on both: (1) your tax bracket (the higher it is, the more you save), and (2) the amount your property has appreciated since purchase (the more it has, the more you save).

Let's work through the figures in the above case. By donating the shares in Fly By Night Productions here's what happens:

One: You save the $324 in capital gains tax you would have had to pay upon sale.

Two: You get a charitable deduction equal to 45 percent tax bracket × $2,000 = $900.

Three: Of course, you're out the $2,000 you would have received from selling the stock.

So the net result is $324 + $900 − $2,000 = $776 that you are out-of-pocket after the donation. But here's the magic: although it cost *you* $776 to *make* the donation, the recipient is ahead *by a full $2,000* (the fair market value of the stock)! You have paid *less than 40 percent* of the actual true value of the gift—and Uncle Sam has paid the rest!!!

Now remember, we hinted before at the fact that the two contribution limits we discussed above might be different for non-cash gifts, and they are. You are limited to deducting appreciated property donations *up to 30 percent* of your adjusted gross income in the year of donation, not 50 percent as in the case of cash gifts. However the five-year carryover that applies in the 50 percent, cash-gift situation, also applies to appreciated-property donations. Just remember that if your recipient is a *private foundation*, you are still stuck with the *20 percent*-of-adjusted-gross income ceiling, and there is *no carryover* allowed.

What kind of "property" qualifies? Most any kind. You can give away securities, as was shown above. (Those securities can be publicly traded, or else stock you own in a "closely held" or "restricted" corporation, in which case the fees for having their worth appraised may also be deductible). You can give away "real property:" *real estate.*

Donations Of Real Estate

Stop right there. Real estate donation is so potentially worthwhile to you, it's worth a momentary digression all its own.

There's that rustic little cabin on a lake that you bought, Tom, before you had even met Tammy. Tammy likes her running water to flow through faucets, not beaver-dams and attic roofs, so you never go near the place anymore; since your marriage you've rented it out when you can, but generally it sits idle. You paid only $1500 for the place 15 years ago, and you'd dearly like to sell it for the $35,000 it was appraised by a licensed expert just last year.

But here's the problem: first of all, you've taken a substantial amount of depreciation on the place (see Chapter 4). Right now, its adjusted basis is down to $750. Second, despite its appraisal value there's not a single potential buyer in sight. And even if you could find one, the local real estate agent has warned you to expect an offer at least 15 percent below appraisal with costly "owner financing" to boot. Oh yeah, the agent: her commission will be 6 percent if the place ever does sell. And *if* it ever *does* sell, your capital gains tax is going to whack the life out of any profit you do realize. In short, you want out—but you can't see any way out.

Hold it! Along comes the Birdwatchers League of Mid-Michigan County, a properly certified tax-exempt public charity. It would dearly love your lakefront paradise for its weekend base of operations. Naturally, the price the League offers you—nothing—seems to leave something to be desired—but does it really?

First—you get the property off your hands. No more maintenance, or rent-related hassles.

Second—you get to decide exactly what day the property changes hands.

Third—no real estate agent commission to be paid. Assuming that charge would have been 6 percent of a $30,000 sales price, you save $1,800.

Fourth—No "owner financing" necessary. Let's just assume that the present value of the owner financing you would have had to give a buyer to realize even a $30,000 price, would have been $3,000. That's how much you save.

Fifth—No no capital gains tax upon profit after sale. Let's say your profit would have been $30,000 − $1,800 agent's commission − $750 adjusted basis = $27,450. Your capital gains tax on this profit would have been $27,450 × .4 capital gains rate × 45 percent tax bracket = $4941. Ugh! By donating instead, all but the recaptured depreciation is *saved*.

Sixth—You get a whopping charitable deduction for the appraised value of $35,000 on your property (provided the appraisal is by a licensed expert and can be fully documented). That deduction is worth $35,000 × .45 tax rate = $15,750 in actual taxes saved. Now remember our 30 percent rule. If you're in the 45 percent marginal tax bracket and you're married, chances are your adjusted gross income is in the $70,000 range. That being the case, you are limited to taking a $23,000 charitable deduction in the year of your donation. The $12,000 balance can be deducted over the following one or two years and up to five, if need be.

Seventh—Because you're donating the property, you are out the hypothetical sales price of $30,000.

So what's the net result? You're out $30,000. But you've saved $1,800 (agent's commission) + $3,000 (owner financing) + $4,941 (capital gains tax) + $15,750 (taxes saved through charitable deduction) − $135 (depreciation recapture) = $4,374 *net cost to you* of making the donation. For a little over four thousand bucks, you have become the philanthropic bigshot of MidMichigan County, having contributed property

worth more than $30,000 to a public cause of your choosing.
Uncle Sam, by the way, has joined in your generosity to the
tune of $4,941 (capital gains tax foregone + $15,750 (actual
taxes saved through charitable deduction) = $20,691.

And note what the foregoing illustration *doesn't* include.
It doesn't include any of the title-transfer and other such
local taxes normally paid by a seller of real property—which,
under the circumstances, the Birdwatchers League may be
only too glad to pay for you. In sum, donating appreciated
capital gain property to a public charity represents an
outstanding opportunity for you to leverage your giving
power to the charity of your choice.

What Property Can You Donate

And finally, back to our list of what sorts of property
you can donate.

It can be personal property too—a car, a typewriter,
whatever. It can be deducted at its retail value if new, but
a special note: if such personal property (i.e., not real estate)
is *appreciated* and *tangible* (i.e., not a right to receive
royalties, or dividends, etc.), than the value of the property
for deduction purposes must be reduced by 40 percent of its
appreciation (that is, the long-term gain that would have been
taxed had it been sold at its fair market value). This reduction applies, however, only when the tangible personal property is to be put to a use unrelated to the purpose or function on which the recipient-group's charitable exemption is
based. So in the latter example, the typewriter—or fur-
nishings for the organization's offices—neither of whch is
appreciated property, would not have to be reduced by 40
percent, but a classic sportscar for the group's subsequent
sale might have to be.

A taxpayer can also donate a *future interest*—such as
the right to own a piece of property after her death. He can
donate *intangible* property: the right to receive proceeds from
a life insurance policy, or to receive royalties paid on a literary
work or patent. He can donate surplus inventory

from a business—but such property is not subject to preferential capital gains treatment when sold, and therefore his deduction would be limited to his cost of the articles contributed. He may engage with a tax-exempt group in what is known as a "bargain sale"—a hybrid donation-sale transaction where the piece of property is "sold" to the charitable group at greatly under fair market value. In most cases part of this transaction is treated for tax purposes as a sale, and part as a contribution, but the rules are complicated enough to warrant having a properly qualified tax advisor set the deal up.

What About Volunteer Work?

Unfortunately, your *time* is *not* donatable. If you volunteer your services one night a week, don't expect the taxman to reward you for it. But you *can* take a deduction for the *legitimate expenses* related to your work directly on behalf of a charitable organization, the best example of which is the cost of gasoline to get you to and from wherever it is you volunteer (and overnight food and lodging costs, if you stay away from home).*

Similarly, the costs associated with the *making* of a charitable donation—appraisal fees, parking and transportation, insurance while in transit, legal and accounting fees in preparation for the transaction—are all deductible as well.

In addition to what we've discussed, there are dozens of specialized ways of giving—through charitable lead trusts, interest-free loans, deferred giving programs—which merit closer investigation if you're in a position to make a more substantial contribution, or if you are in the process of providing for your family's needs after your death (either by will, or through the creation of various trusts). These are also

---

* Sorry, costs attributable to day care for your children while you volunteer don't qualify. But if you care for *someone else's children* on behalf of a charitable organization, your unreimbursed expenses will be deductible, provided you have no profit-motive for doing so and aren't paid to do so.

useful devices if you find that your annual giving exceeds the percentage-of-adjusted-gross-income limits discussed above on a regular basis, so that the five-year carryover provision is of no particular use to you.

Donor-Advised Funds

Okay. It's December 15. You see a commercial for one of those tax services on TV and it suddenly occurs to you that you're in for quite an income-tax bite—more like a chomp—this year. Then up pops the nightly news, with yuletime tidings about an Administration plan to spend untold millions to base the MX missile on 1200 miles of abandoned Northeast corridor train track. Thunderstruck, you determine that you've *got* to reduce your tax bill substantially. You've got to help support some organization dedicated to the cause of world peace and disarmament; but you have no earthly idea which group that is. What do you do?

You act, the very next morning, to establish a *donor-advised fund.* A donor-advised fund will do all of the following things for you:

• It will allow you to use *its own* grant-making capabilities as a single, already established charitable organization, to contribute to a whole slew of other charitable organizations which support your cause, but which you simply don't have time to identify and make contact with before the end of the tax year.

• It will permit you to have part or all of your contribution passed-through to *non*-tax-exempt organizations, which are neither 501(c)(3), nor have their own tax-exempt fiscal sponsor. (Of course, the restriction that the funds so distributed still be devoted to a charitable purpose within the exempt purpose of the public charity which is passing through the money, still applies.)

• It will greatly facilitate a contribution of appreciated property other than cash. You simply make *one* lump-sum transfer of the property to the fund; it converts it to cash and distributes that cash to other organizations according to your wishes.

• It will allow you to make donations (up to the amount you put in the fund) to the organizations you target over a period of days, months or years—but get a deduction for the *total* amount in the fund *right away*.

•It will allow you to make contributions *anonymously* to the groups you ultimately target. Any regular contributor to such causes knows that anonymity will greatly reduce one's intake of unsolicited mail.

• It will permit you to have someone else—the fund— handle your recordkeeping chores for you. And depending on the fund, you may ask for and be provided with a list of every existing organization that meets the criteria you set for your support.

There are numerous national community finds around the country that are willing to act as the sponsor for your own donor-advised fund. Given that time is likely to be of the essence, contact your bank, savings-and-loan or credit union officers to seek out the name of some you can contact right away. Or write the Funding Exchange (135 East 15th Street, New York, NY 10013) for assistance. Remember two caveats about this charitable giving device: First, once the fund is created and money is put in, that money is considered "contributed," and you can't get it back. Second, the groups which ultimately receive your support through the fund must fit within the general purpose of the organization which hosts your fund, and each contribution must be approved by that organization's board. So make sure when you create the fund, that your general giving priorities, and those of the host-charity, are well in tune with one another.

Then deduct away.

8

Conserving Farmland—and Tax Dollars Too

When tillage begins, other arts follow. The farmers therefore are the founders of human civilization.

Daniel Webster, 1840

Of all the mighty nations, in the east or in the west,
O this glorious Yankee nation, is the greatest and the best.
We have room for all creation, and our banner is unfurled,
Here's a general invitation to the people of the world:
Uncle Sam is rich enough To give us all a farm.

"Uncle Sam's Farm"
19th Century song

Whatever tempted you and Tammy to buy that 10 acre "farmette" anyway? The allure of manure? The earthly pleasures of earthy plowshares? Your real estate agent insists the fair market value of the place is a tidy sum indeed, but neither he nor you can come up with a buyer "imaginative" enough to divine the same delight in the property that you once did.

All right. Your farm may be an "unproductive asset" for the moment, to be kind, but from a tax point of view it could hold a unique benefit for you, all in the name of the noble cause of conservation.

There are four main actions you might consider taking which would get all (or some) of the farm off your hands. The first three essentially involve giving it away. First, as with any asset, you might consider giving your *entire* ("fee simple") interest in the farm away to a properly qualified charity that for reasons beknownst only to it wants the place. You

Deduct This Book

might consider giving away to a charity some undivided *portion* of your entire interest—say, a 20 percent interest in the full ten abominable acres. Third, you might consider donating a *remainder interest*—that is, the right to full (or partial) ownership in the farm when the lives of the current owners terminate. (The latter is known to scare some would-be donors who believe it gives powerful philanthropic institutions an incentive to accelerate their death.) The tax advantages of appreciated property donations generally are discussed in Chapter 7.

But there is a fourth alternative open to you and it's unique to farmland. It was made possible by changes to the tax laws enacted by Congress in 1980, and it could permit you—if your property meets a set of qualifications—to go on "enjoying" your Greenacres while reaping greenbacks from Uncle Sam. You would be making a "qualified conservation contribution" (QCC). And it works like this.

How Qualified Conservation Contributions Work

First, we must identify the right recipient. This part is easy. The law specifies that to qualify, your "grantee" must be a government, a public charity, or some other charity which is controlled by a unit of government or by a public charity. A prime candidate is a three-year old conservation group based in Washington, D.C., called the American Farmland Trust (AFT), which specializes in receiving exactly what you, Tom and Tammy, would dearly love to give.

Second, we define the "thing" it is you would be donating. You would be giving the AFT either an *easement* (which is the right to use your property in a specified manner), or a *restrictive covenant* (the right to prohibit your property from being used in a certain manner). The goal of the donation is to conserve your farmland in its present form. Hence, a typical donated restrictive covenant would give AFT the right to prevent any development of your farmland other than for agricultural purposes, or to limit any further development to uses in conformity with prevailing agricultural zoning restrictions.

Such a donation would in many instances have a "value" attached to it. And that value would, predictably enough, equal the difference between the fair market value of your property as it exists today, and its fair market value with the donated restriction in place. Of course, if your land abuts a billion dollar hotel-shopping-mall-office-center complex, or edges near a sprawling suburban community whose developers are paying courtesy calls on you hourly, the restrictive convenant could have very considerable value. And in such a situation, your conservationist impulses may be overcome by an itch to actually sell your land and retire to Maui for the rest of your life. But presuming you have no such good fortune, your would-be donated easement may still be sufficiently "valuable" (without being commercially salable) to make the donation very worthwhile to you *from a tax viewpoint.*

Third, your contribution under the law must be made *exclusively for conservation purposes.* Key to meeting this test is the wording of the easement or covenant you grant; with a little lawerly assistance, the proper language (eg., "preservation of open space") won't be hard to find.

Fourth, your donation must be made *for the scenic enjoyment of the general public,* or *pursuant to a clearly delineated federal, state or local governmental conservation or preservation policy.* Take the "scenic enjoyment" test first: does this mean that you must contend with gawkers of all shapes and sizes trampling across upon your prized acreage by the busload? No—physical access to the property is not required, and visual access is enough. As to the alternative, "governmental policy" test, the best bet is to obtain some sort of certification by a government agency—federal, state or local—that granting your easement or covenant would in fact further its preservation or conservation policies. Working with your prospective grantee on this aspect of the grant should simplify things considerably.

Regardless of which of the two tests above you choose to meet, there is the further requirement that your grant yield *a significant public benefit*. This may be the toughest test to hurdle: if your piece of land is ordinary in every respect (again, your would-be grantee can tell you), you may have some difficulties. But if it has unique characteristics (eg., the only cotton plantation in Connecticut), or is potentially threatened by development, or is of such nature that preserving it would be consistent with a public conservation-preservation program, it ought not to be a problem demonstrating that your grant will yield a "significant public benefit."

Finally, recognize now that your grant, once given, is *forever*. It applies not just to you, Tom and Tammy, but to *any future owner* of the land (hence the value of the easement or convenant in the first place).

What's Your QCC Worth?

So you meet each of the criteria set forth above—what now? Now, have an independent appraiser familiar with land values in your area appraise the land as is, and as it would be worth following your donation. Let's say the fair market value of the land as is, appraises at $50,000, and as after your donation, at $40,000. The difference of $10,000 represents the value of your donation.

That $10,000 represents a tax-deductible charitable contribution for you, within certain limits. The tax laws provide that a taxpayer's gifts of "appreciated property" (generally, property that could have been sold for profits recognized as long-term capital gains) may be deducted at their fair market value up to 30 percent of the taxpayer's "contribution base" (which is generally "adjusted gross income," your gross income minus the expenses of earning it) for that particular year. Hence, if your adjusted gross income in 1983, the year of the donation, is $33,400 or more and you have no other charitable contributions falling into the same tax-category, then you will get the full $10,000 deduction in 1982.

Assuming further that you fall into the 30 percent marginal tax bracket, that deduction will be worth almost $.3 \times \$10,000 = \$3,000$ to you in actual tax savings. Should you have earned less than $33,400, or should you have other donations as well, then the balance over $10,000 may be "carried over" and applied against the taxes you owe in each of five succeeding tax years (subject to the same 30 percent ceiling in each year).

There is one slight drawback to be aware of. Inasmuch as you have contributed away a portion of the value of your property, you have lowered its value, and that "reduction in basis" must be factored in when calculating taxable profit at the time of sale. (This "basis reduction rule" is the same as with regard to preservation easements, discussed in Chapter 10.)

One further warning: seek very careful guidance regarding the recipient of your grant. Make sure that it fits the eligibility tests described above, and particularly that it is not a "private foundation"—because if it is, you'll recall, much stricter limits than the 30 percent/five-year carryover apply.

9

The Rehabilitation Tax Incentives— Preservation For Profit

The historic buildings in a community are tangible links with the nation's past that help provide a sense of identity and stability that is most often missing in this era of constant change.... President Reagan's program for economic recovery calls for major new [tax] initiatives to stimulate private investment in rehabilitation that will enhance the existing preservation incentives. As the cornerstone of the Administration's nationwide preservation program, the new incentives will help maximize private capital, create new jobs and bring about economic revitalization. The [Interior] Department is committed to acting quickly to implement the new provisions [of the 1981 Economic Recovery Tax Act].

Interior Secretary James G. Watt
November, 1981

The Reagan Administration, as expected, "zeroed out" historic preservation grants to the states and to the National Trust [for Historic Preservation]. That recommendation is contained in the Federal budget for the 1983 fiscal year....

Article in *Preservation News*
The newspaper of the National Trust for Historic Preservation
March, 1982

If the quotes above strike you as curiously contradictory, relax, because they are both, curious and contradictory. But then, so is the wave of real-estate rehabilitation fever sweeping the nation.

Consider:

• That from coast to coast, large, hard-to-maintain turn-of-the-century mansions which would have been thought prime albatross targets for the wrecker's ball just a few years ago, are suddenly prized for conversion into office buildings, residential condominiums and—yes, even rental apartments.

• That the man most singly responsible for our national swing to suburbia some time ago, megadeveloper James Rouse, now tells awed audiences of attorneys, architects, realtors and planners, "There are wonderful old buildings that are waiting to be restored . . . . An old and beautiful building has a value that can't be captured or matched by new construction."

• That owner-developers of a 730-acre community on Nevada's Lake Tahoe, where a shorefront foot fetches many times its length in solid gold chain, opted to preserve many of its landmark farmhouse-style buildings, instead of constructing sprawling lakeside condominia.

• That the number of state and local preservation commissions—entities with power to certify a particular building or district as "historic"—jumped from 578 in 1978 to 832 in 1981, while the number of listings in the National Register of Historic Places more than doubled from 13,000 to 27,000 between 1977-1982.

• That the American Institute of Architects estimates about 77 percent of *all* building activity across the U.S. in 1982 was in reconstruction and rehabilitation. Half of New York City's 1982 budget for capital outlays was devoted to rehabilitation.

• That whatever these new tax incentives for rehabilitation are, a series of technical seminars about them, sponsored by the National Trust for Historic Preservation, drew about 4,000 persons paying up to $150 apiece.

In Oakland, California, city fathers reportedly have sold the Oakland Museum to private investors who have leased it back to the city and will let them re-purchase it again, after it is renovated into a theater complex. In San Antonio, Texas, the long-vacant century-old Lone Star Brewery is now, following a four-year-long $9 million restoration, the dramatic new home of the San Antonio Museum of Art, and locals call it the town's "Cinderella story."

Well you bought this book to read about how to save taxes, not fairy tales. But the cause of so much of this new activity, the rehabilitation tax incentives spawned by the 1981 Economic Recovery Tax Act (ERTA), are something of a fairy tale after all: because of them, instead of paying your hard-earned money to harden a nuclear-tipped missile silo somewhere, you can instead opt to give a decaying income property a new lease on life, *and* profit nicely doing so. In fact, using the tax incentives right may not only wipe out all the federal income taxes you owe this year, but give you a whopping *refund* of taxes you paid *last* year . . . . and the year before that, and the year before *that*. Now that *is* a Progressive-minded taxpayer's fantasy dream-come-true, so read on.

The Three Rehabilitation Tax Incentives

In ERTA, Congress substantially changed the tax treatment given persons who rehabilitate historic structures, or else non-historic ones above a certain age and in certain situations. What it did was create a set of three income tax credits, which work like this:

I. If the owner of a building between *30 and 39* years old "substantially rehabilitates" it for a *commercial* purpose, then the rehabilitation costs she incurs are eligible for a *15 percent* federal income tax credit;

II. If the building is *at least 40* years old, and is "substantially rehabilitated" for a *commercial* purpose, then the credit goes up to *20 percent;*

III. If the building qualifies as a *certified historic structure,* and is substantially rehabilitated in accordance with guidelines laid down by the government applicable to historic preservation, then—regardless of whether the property is put to a *commercial or residential rental* use—the rehabilitation costs qualify for a 25 percent credit.

That is a bare-bones description of the three new credits. Now let's label them Credits I, II and III, respectively, and take a more detailed look at each of them.

Just one word before we begin: *don't* just stop reading because you're not a builder, can't tell a joist from a rivet and don't care to learn. Read on anyway, and once you get through all the technical complexities of the credits you will see how they can still be *extremely useful to you.*

The Two Commercial Use Credits

Credits I and II are conceptually identical, beyond the building-age distinction. First of all, to qualify for the 15 or 20 percent credits, the rehabilitation work you engage in must enable the completed structure to be used for a *commercial purpose.* If it becomes an office (and the applicable zoning laws allow it), that is fine; a factory is fine too. A rental apartment building or condominium project is *not* fine— make *absolutely* sure, therefore, that the building you decide to give a new lease on life to *will* be able to be put to a bonafide commercial purpose.

Substantial Rehabilitation

Next, the rehabilitation you undertake must be *substantial.* Your idea of what is "substantial" (backbreaking labor; wasted weekends) is not the taxman's, and it is the latter that counts. "Substantial" is defined two ways, and your project must meet *both* definitions: (1) the "external wall" test, and (2) the "adjusted basis or $5,000" test.

The "external wall" test is simple: after your project is rehabilitated, 75 percent of the buildings's original external walls must still be in place, as external walls. Note: this *doesn't* mean that three out of four walls have to remain perfectly intact while you bulldoze the fourth; it does mean that three-fourths of the *total area* (length times height) of all four walls, including window and door spaces, must still be standing as outside walls when you're done.

The other, "adjusted basis or $5,000" test is a bit more complicated. It says that the *cost* of the rehabilitation work you do must, over a maximum 24 month period, *exceed* the *greater* of: (a) the building's "adjusted basis" (excluding land), or (b) $5,000.

Best to explain this two-pronged test by example: say you buy a commercially zoned property for $15,000, including the price of the land. Your first step, as with all income property, is to allocate a share of the purchase price to the value of the land (which you cannot depreciate) and to the value of the structure (which you can—see Chapter 4). So let's assume that the land value is 50 percent, or $7,500. We subtract that from the price, leaving $7,500 as the depreciable "basis." Now—to qualify for Credit I (if your building is between 30-39 years old) or Credit II (if it's 40-plus years old), the rehabilitation job must cost *at least* $7,500. (Note that the lower, $5,000 "threshold" doesn't come into play here, because it is lower than the "basis.") Now suppose, instead, that you've owned the property for two years, and have taken depreciation to the point where your "adjusted basis" has dropped to $4,500. All well and good, but now, to qualify for either credit, your rehabilitation work must cost *at least* $5,000 (the $4,500 figure has become irrelevant because the $5,000 "threshold" is higher). Get the picture?

So 75 percent of your external wall-space is left intact, and the cost of the job satisfies the "adjusted basis or $5,000" test. You're chomping at the bit—what next?

Work Done Since Jan. 1, '82

Next, to qualify for the credit, your rehabilitation work must have been done *since* January 1, 1982. This is because the law granting the new incentives, passed in 1981, was written to encourage *new* rehabilitation work, not to reward a windfall to those who did it beforehand anyway. In the event you began work on a rehabilitation project before January 1, 1982 but didn't complete it by then, then you must apportion the costs of work as pre-January 1 and post-January 1, and treat them for tax purposes under prior and present law respectively. We'll assume, to keep it simple, that your involvement will be with a project that got underway in 1982 or 1983.

Wait a minute—are we saying that *all* rehabilitation costs qualify? No—but pretty darn near, and that's one of the most amazing things about each of these credits as we'll soon see. For now, let's assume that the rehabilitation costs associated with your commercial-purpose project total $100,000, meeting both "substantial" tests above. That means, in effect, that you're entitled to a tax credit, equal to $15,000 (if the building was 30-39 years old) or $20,000 (if 40-plus years old). In other words, you are entitled to reduce the actual federal income taxes you owe, dollar-for-dollar, by $15,000 or $20,000, respectively.

A New Chance To Get Back Old Taxes

"Woah," you say. "I owe *nowhere near* $15,000 in taxes this year—and if I did, I'd pay a full-time accountant to do my taxes and wouldn't be reading this book!" Herein lies the big secret of the rehabilitation tax incentives, that single characteristic that makes them *so* worthwhile, *especially* to lower-bracket taxpayers, that none in their right mind ought let the opportunity pass.

The secret to the rehabilitation tax credit is this: that portion of the credit which you don't use up ("absorb") this year, you can "carry back" up to three years, and "carry forward" up to 15 years! In layman's terms, you can get a whopping refund of thousands of tax dollars you *already paid*, and thought were lost to you forever.

Consider the $15,000 credit of a moment ago. Suppose that after taking into account all exemptions, deductions and other reductions in taxable income, you will owe Uncle Sam $7,000 this year. Your $15,000 credit is first applied against this year's income tax and so you end up owing nothing. (That's right, *nothing* . . . . and if you've been withholding through your employer, *every cent* of it will come back to you once you file.) That leaves you a residual credit of $8,000. Now, retrieve your federal income tax return from three years ago (in this case, let's assume it's for tax year 1980). If you can't find it, simply call your IRS regional office and they'll send you a copy. You see that you paid $3,000 tax that year; apply the residual credit and you will be eligible for a *full* refund of that $3000. Next, look at tax year 1981. You've still got a credit for $5,000 coming, so if you paid $4,000 in 1981, that comes back as a full refund also, leaving you a $1,000 credit to be applied against taxes paid in tax year 1982. Now suppose you paid no taxes that year. You will hold onto the credit—just "store" it in your closet like a favorite piece of warm winter clothing—until tax year 1984 rolls around, at which time you will be entitled to offset those taxes by the remaining credit. You will be able to apply whatever credit remains up to 15 years in the future, that is, until and including tax year 1997!

Set The Treasury A' Trembling

Note what is going on here. Not only have you acquired the ability to "zero out" whatever income taxes you owe in the *present* year, and thereby deprive the Administration of the fruits of your present income. You have *also* discovered how to relieve the Treasury of those moneys you've paid into the system *during the last three years.* Imagine the effect upon the federal budgeteers of the world, were 10 million law-abiding, taxpaying Americans suddenly to request a refund of *all* the federal income taxes they paid since 1980! And note how democratic it is: the credit affects all who take advantage of it equally, regardless of whether you're a 50 percent bracket $250,000 a year earner, or a 35 percent bracket $30,000 earner, *so long as* you paid taxes in the past, are paying them now, or will pay them in the future. Robin Hood and his merrymen could not do better—plus this little operation is *perfectly legal.*

Possible Recapture

So what's the downside, you're gasping? One downside—and it's a minor one, considering the advantages—is that the credit may be subject to "recapture" in two ways. It is subject to outright, proportional recapture if you sell your property within five years after you place it into post-rehabilitation service. To illustrate: if you get a $15,000 credit, that credit would have to be paid back to the government in one-fifth increments for each year less than five in which the building is sold. If you sell it one year after putting it into service, you owe the IRS four-fifths of $15,000 or $12,000; if you sell it two years later, you owe three-fifths of $15,000 or $9,000, and so on. Once you wait more than five years, the credit is yours in full.

The second manner in which the credit is subject to recapture is through the effect it has on the depreciable basis of your property. Normally, given that you paid, let's say, $30,000 for your property and put $100,000 into rehabilitating it, and the land-value is put at $15,000, your basis would be $30,000 + $100,000 − $15,000 = $115,000. But a special rule applicable to the commercial 15 percent and 20 percent credits requires you to *lower* the basis by the full amount of the credit, so that in this case, your basis would actually be $115,000 − $15,000 credit = $100,000.

How does this affect you? It depends on your tax-bracket; the higher your bracket, the more it affects you. Recall that "basis" is the measure for the amount you can depreciate every year (again, refer to Chapter 4 for a full discussion of depreciation), and so the lower your basis, the less you can depreciate. Secondly, the "adjusted basis" (original basis plus capital improvements minus depreciation) is the measure against which you will calculate the taxable "profit" you make at the time you ultimately sell: the lower the basis, the higher the "profit," and the more tax you pay. But also keep in mind that you will be taxed on that "profit" at much lower *capital-gains* rates, whereas the credit you earn *now* acts to cancel out income tax you owe at *ordinary-income* rates.

Slower Depreciation

A second downside concerns the *rate* at which you are allowed to depreciate the property. Again, the severity of this downside is related directly to your tax bracket. As we discussed before, the 1981 Economic Recovery Tax Act greatly enhanced the value of income-producing real estate by: (1) allowing owners to depreciate a newly acquired property over a "recovery period" of 15 years, instead of the much longer typical 25-40 year period in the old law; and (2) allowing an owner to elect to take "accelerated depreciation" (more speedy depreciation during the early years of ownership) in lieu of "straight line" depreciation (a rate that stays constant every month over the property's life). Now, when one takes the rehabilitation tax credit, the option of taking accelerated depreciation is forfeited and one is stuck with *having to use* straight-line for *that portion of your basis attributable to the rehabilitation costs* (the portion attributable to original acquisition is still eligible for acceleration). This affects the stream of depreciation deductions you can take, but the affect is much greater if your tax bracket is higher. Also, keep in mind that in the event you take accelerated depreciation, upon sale of the property, the excess of that depreciation over that which would have been taken under the straight-line method, is recapturable at the higher, ordinary income rate.

The net effect of all of the above gobbledygook is that the relative advantages of the credits are *greater* for taxpayers in *lower* brackets. Couple this fact with the fact that lower-income taxpayers tend not to have taken proper advantage of all the tax breaks available to them in past years . . . . and you have the makings of real tax manna for the masses here.

The Historic Rehabilitation Credit

Now let's turn to Credit III, the 25 percent tax credit applicable to historic rehabilitation. It has several features distinguishing it from the first two:

• **Commercial or Residential Use**—As we said before, Credit III is applicable to any form of "depreciable property," that is, property owned as an income-producing investment, and *not as the residence* of the owner or a family-member. Whether it's a commercial-use or residential-use investment *doesn't matter* for Credit III.

• **Certified Historic Structure**—Credit III is available only when the building being rehabilitated is a *certified historic structure.* The law defines two sorts of historic structures: (A) any property listed individually in the National Register of Historic Places; and (B) a property located within a "registered historic district"—an area which is itself listed in the National Register, or which is designated historic by a state or local body with authority to do so. All properties in category A are automatically "certified historic," but those in category B must be individually certified.

This individual certification process is pretty straightforward, and it's tied to one overall criterion: that the building in question contribute to the "historic significance" of the district it's in. This will virtually always be the case if the building, " . . . . by location, design, setting, materials, workmanship, feeling and association adds to the district's sense of time and place and historic development." It will almost always *not* be the case if the building *detracts* from the district's historic significance; or "where the integrity of the original design or individual architectural features or spaces have been irretrievably lost or . . . . where physical deterioration and/or structural damage has not made it reasonably feasible to rehabilitate the building." And certification is most *unlikely* if the structure is less than 50 years old, unless its "historical or architectural merit" are especially strong, or the historic attributes of the district itself are less than 50 years old.

If all of this seems prohibitively convoluted, sit back and rejoice in the fact that during the first quarter of 1982—the first three months of operation of the new credit—415 of 459 requests for certification of structures in historic districts were approved. That's a better than 90 percent batting average. And if you're smart about how you approach certification—by making sure that a building you have your eye on is in a historic district; by checking certification even before you buy—you shouldn't have any problem clearing this hurdle.

• **Qualified Rehabilitation**—In addition to the rehabilitation of the structure having to be "substantial," as for Credits I and II, in the case of Credit III it must also be *qualified.* A "qualified substantial rehabilitation" is one where, in addition to meeting the "external wall" and "greater of adjusted basis or $5,000" tests discussed above, the rehabilitation process itself must follow detailed standards set forth by the Department of Interior.*

• **Basis Adjustment**—Just like Credits I and II, any surplus of Credit III remaining after you pay this year's tax can be carried back three years, and forward 15 years. An important distinction, though, is in the way taking Credit III *affects the basis* of your rehabilitated property. Recall that we said, as to Credits I and II, that the basis of the structure must be adjusted downward by the *full* amount of the credit, thereby affecting the size of your monthly depreciation allowances, and also of the taxable "profit" you realize upon sale. That is also true for Credit III—but only *partially* so. It goes like this:

— If you rehabilitated your historic structure and "placed it into service" (used it in trade or business, or put it up for rent) *before* January 1, 1983, *no adjustment whatsoever* need have been made to the building's basis. (For instance, if the building cost you $20,000 exclusive of land, and your rehabilitation costs came to $100,000, your basis would have remained at a full $120,000, despite your eligibility for a $25,000 federal income tax credit.)

---

* These standards pertain to such aspects of the process as, for instance, making "every reasonable effort" to use the building for its originally intended purpose; preserving "distinctive stylistic features;" repairing rather than replacing deteriorated but historically relevant features, and so on. The Department's Technical Preservation Services Division issues a continual stream of bulletins interpreting these standards as they affect particular physical elements of the rehabilitation process, such as enclosures, storefront alterations and the like.)

—If the building is placed in service *on or after* January 1, 1983, then the basis must be reduced by *one-half* of the allowable credit. (In the above example, the basis would become $20,000 cost + $100,000 capital improvements −(½ × $25,000 credit) = $107,500.)

Just as for Credits I and II, depreciation deductions for that portion of the basis allocated to the rehabilitation can be taken only straight-line, i.e., in equal increments over the 15-year long recovery period. And Credit III, like its brothers, is subject to proportional outright recapture if sale occurs during the first five years following rehabilitation.

• **Which Costs Qualify**—Now we return to that matter we glossed over earlier: which expenses associated with rehabilitating an historic or non-historic property, will actually qualify as subject to the credits? Given how broad the answer seems to be, it's easier to ask which costs are *not* allowed. Not eligible for the credits are: (1) the cost of buying the building (or land) in the first place; (2) the costs associated with *enlarging* the structure beyond its existing total volume, and (3) the cost of carpeting, draperies, office equipment, furniture (even where it is built-in), non-permanent (demountable) walls or partitions, and other similar items of personal property; (4) interest paid on loans which supply the funds for rehabilitation (so-called "construction-period interest"), and (4) costs relating to the land (such as landscaping) rather than the structure.

The remaining allowable costs are based on rules the IRS issued under the old law applying to rehabilitation costs for historic structures. It is conceivable that the IRS will issue new rules, maybe even different ones distinguishing allowable costs for Credits I, II and III. But for the time being, developers and investors across the land are relying on the current, expansive definition of which costs are allowable. And how expansive it is! Included as eligible, for instance, are:

• Expenditures for "modernization," including such amenities as modern plumbing and electrical wiring, heating and air conditioning, elevators and escalators and improvements required to meet local building and fire codes. In the case of Credit III, these costs are allowed provided they are incurred as part of the certified rehabilitation, and are "consistent with the historic character of the structure."

• In the case of Credit III, the costs of "re-locating" a certified historic structure to another locale, so long as the re-location is expressly approved by the Interior Secretary or designee.

• Expenditures for demolishing a part of the structure (provided the "exterior wall" test is still met, as well as any historic-rehabilitation guidelines).

• Expenditures for "architectural and engineering fees, real estate commissions, site-survey fees, legal expenses, insurance premiums, developers' fees and other construction-related costs."

How You Can Use The Credits

So much for all the technical details on how the three rehabilitation tax credits work in theory. We promised you could apply them to your own situation, and there are two ways to make these credits work for you: the hard way and the easy way.

The hard way is to don your hard hat and dive into the rubble. If you're a history buff, an unemployed handyperson or an occupational masochist, that's the way to go. But there are substantial pitfalls: you'll have to raise rehabilitating funds at high interest rates; you may encounter costly obstacles to the job you never anticipated, and so on. Tax-saving is always a good idea . . . . but, it just may not be worth the effort.

But then there's the easy way, which involves a feature of the credits we haven't looked at yet. The easy way is to let a professional developer do the dirty work, then buy his finished product and have his credit "pass on" to you. The chances are you would like to know more about the easy way, and we'll take a detailed illustration as our example.*

During the 1970's, a real estate developer with considerable savvy bought, in conjunction with a group of investors, a 20-unit apartment building located in a registered D.C. historic district. He obtained all necessary permits to convert the building to a 20-unit condominium, each of them one-bedroom. Before he turned a single spade, the developer sought out and received a personal inspection of the property from a representative of the District of Columbia's Historic Preservation Office (HPO).

The representative bestowed her blessing on his plans to rehabilitate the project: of primary historic significance were the building's marble lobby and oakwood handrails on stairs throughout the building, which the developer undertook to return as near as possible to their original state. Then he went to work: each unit received a new refurbished fireplace, its own heat-pump (and central air conditioning), washer-dryer, dishwasher and all new kitchen appliances and cabinetry, etc. Total allowable rehabilitation costs on the building (as we've outlined above) came to roughly $1 million, making the developer and his investor-co-owners eligible for a $250,000 historic rehabilitation tax credit, upon certification of his work by the appropriate Interior Department officials.

The team then faced a hard choice: whether to keep the credit to themselves, or "pass it on" to prospective buyers of the individual units. Now note: were those buyers to become owner-occupiers, they would *not* be eligible for the credit—it only applies to "depreciable property," which does not include one's own residence. So the developer devised a marketing plan aimed at would-be buyer-investors, and made the pass-on credit a central element of his marketing strategy.

Putting a price on those 20 different units was the next critical step in the developer's plan of action, and it was here that he and his preservation-savvy accountant displayed

---

* This example borrows from several different actual case studies in order to illustrate the full potential benefits involved.

their genius. First, they secured commitments from a local savings-and-loan to provide financing for their buyer-investors with "ten percent down" (i.e., an investor would have to put up ten percent of the purchase price at the time of settlement). Next, they calculated what typical settlement costs—loan origination fees, title transfer taxes, a year's setting aside of property taxes and insurance, etc.—would be, and found that typical settlement would cost the buyer about 5 percent of the purchase price.

Now it was time to set the asking prices, and they set them such that the federal income tax rehabilitation credit passed on to the buyer of each unit would *almost precisely* *"cancel out"* the ten percent down payment-plus five percent settlement costs the buyer would have to come up with at settlement time! In other words, someone buying a $60,000 one-bedroom unit in the building would also be buying a $9,000 income tax credit—a refund of $9,000 on her taxes—that would cancel out the funds ($6,000 downpayment plus $3,000 settlement charges) she'd need to to have to buy the unit in the first place. All the buyer would have to do, then, would be to come up with the funds in order to purchase the unit some time in 1982, include the credit on her 1982 tax return, get the $9,000 refund (from this year's taxes or earlier years, as explained above), and "pay herself back" her original investment. The buyer would then own her unit outright, just like any "straight" real-estate investment— the crucial difference being that her $6,000 "equity" in the unit (the portion of its cost already paid for) was paid for *entirely* out of a tax refund!!! To knock the point home with a sledgehammer: the buyer here would increase her net worth by $6,000 *instantly* and *completely* at Uncle Sam's expense.

There are more tax advantages to come. The developer is arranging for a donation of a facade easement on the property (see Chapter 10). And of course, all the normal tax benefits associated with real estate investments, such as the deductibility of settlement costs and depreciation, applied to this project as well. (Keep in mind, however, that once again the portion of each unit's basis associated with its rehabilitation can be depreciated over the 15 year recovery period using only the straight-line method.)

But why should the developer and his buddies be willing to give up such a lucrative credit? Because, dear Tom and Tammy, despite the dismal real estate climate affecting most real-estate pros, they managed to make out like bandits. The prices they put on their units worked out to approximately $100 per-square-foot—not out of line, but substantially higher than the $75 per square foot "fire sales" other builders were forced into around Washington. The financing their buyers obtained was at the going market interest rate, meaning that the developer, unlike virtually all his starving colleagues, was not forced to "buy down" a loan rate (pay the lender a lot of cash as "interest-in-advance" in exchange for low-rate loans). And the units sold so fast, by word-of-mouth, that he was not forced to "carry" his completed units at heavy construction-period interest rates for any appreciable amount of time. It was, for him, a project-dream-come-true. And it was for his unit buyers an unbeatable opportunity to direct federal funds away from densely packed missiles and other similarly offensive expenditures into their *very own, socially productive, highly profitable investment* without getting any dirt on their hands.

Where profitable tax-advantaged investment opportunities lie, limited partnership tax shelters soon follow. One such partnership—oil and gas drilling—is described in more detail in Chapter 11; essentially they permit you to participate in a potentially profitable activity, and share in the accompanying tax benefits, without risking anything beyond the amount of your initial commitment of funds to the partnership. Given the attractiveness of the rehabilitation tax credits, you can expect to see a rapidly growing selection of such shelters offering the chance to take part in major real estate re-development projects, and share in the credits just described, without having to take over actual ownership of the property yourself. These offerings are certainly worth checking out—but make absolutely sure before you jump at a particular project that the principals behind it— the so-called "general partners"—are financially reputable, *and* have a solid base of experience in the rehabilitation field.

Two final points ought to be made about the rehabilitation tax credits. The first is that *long-term lessees* of rehabilitated property may also take advantage of the credit, provided that the lease extends for at least 15 years from the date the rehabilitation is completed, and no owner has taken the credit herself.

The second point applies only to taxpayers whose investment tax credits of all types are particularly large in a single year. The 1982 Tax Equity and Fiscal Responsibility Act set a new limit on the amount of income tax liability that may be offset in any year by investment tax credits, at 85 percent of income in excess of $25,000. In other words, if you're eligible for a $20,000 rehabilitation credit at the end of 1983, and have sufficient 1983 tax liability to offset it, you can offset the whole thing. If your credit is for $35,000 you may offset $25,000 + (85% × $10,000) = $33,500, leaving you $1,500 in unused 1983 credits. Of course, you can still reduce your remaining income by other, non-credit tax deductions. And you can still carry backward up to three years the $1,500 balance of the credit you couldn't use this year. Accordingly, to taxpayers in middle-income categories this credit-limit provision is really no big deal.

So much for the rehabilitation tax incentives. Let Congressional votes on the MX missile, B-1 bomber and Clinch River reactor fall where they may; as long as there's a building left standing in these United States which is worthy of repair and rejuvenation, *you* don't have to pick up the tab for these and other national nightmares if *you* don't want to. For the beleagured, moderate-income taxpayer who's paid taxes up to the gills for the last three years . . . . who's looking for a good investment but doesn't have ready cash to invest . . . . who would like to "zero out" the taxes he owes, this year, legally and cleanly . . . . these credits represent a new New Deal. Use them, and use them well.

10

Preservation Easements— Put The Wealth Of History In Your Pocket

The rehabilitation tax credits described in the preceding chapter apply, we said, only to property held for the production of income—i.e., not to your own residence. But there is another tax benefit associated with preserving the historic character of a piece of property, which you can qualify for regardless of *whether you live in it or not,* and it, too, can make a distinct difference in the taxes you pay.

This benefit is called a *preservation easement.* It will take a little bit of explaining to clarify just what this animal is, whether your property could qualify, and what that fact would mean to your own tax situation.

An "easement" is a term of law used to signify an interest, or right, in a piece of property which its owner transfers to another while retaining ownership of the property itself. For example, if you grant your next-door neighbor the right to cross your land in order to get to a lake on the other side, you have given your neighbor an easement. In theory, and usually in practice as well, this easement carries a monetary value—whatever the convenience of being able to cross your land is "worth," in this case. And, your land is, at least in theory, decreased in value by the worth of the right you have transferred away. It is in this transfer of value that the tax considerations of easements come into play.

A preservation easement involves the transferring away of *some* of your normal rights, as a property owner, to modify the *historic* character of the structures on your land. More precisely, what you transfer away when you grant a preservation easement is the right to demolish the building, or to modify its essential exterior appearance—and that is all. You still own the property, and can change its interior, rent it, sell it, have raucous parties inside it, etc. But the easement is forever—"into perpetuity," the law calls it—and it "runs with the land" in legalese, meaning that its restriction applies to any future owners of the property too.

What's A Preservation Easement Worth?

So what is such a preservation easement on your property worth? Let's quote L'Enfant Trust, a Washington, D.C.—based non-profit outfit formed to receive such easements and a foremost authority on the subject: "In general, the value of the donated easement is equal to the diminution [decrease] of the property's fair market value attributable to the easement (the fair market value of the property after the easement is donated). When determining this value for tax purposes, there are numerous factors to consider—the restrictions imposed by the easement, the nature and location of the property, the applicable zoning, the likelihood of development, and others—all matters within the purview of a competent appraiser."

Huh?

Let's take some simple examples. If the property under consideration for an easement is a one-bedroom, one-story house on a two-acre lot zoned for intensive commercial development, and the local historic-preservation authorities have no problem with its being razed to make way for a 40-floor hotel-office complex, rest assured your preservation easement has substantial value—far more value, perhaps, than the building sitting there right now. At the other extreme, take a 20-unit apartment building just converted to condominiums, on a piece of land where other forms of development would neither make sense nor be permitted under current zoning ordinances. The chances that this building's exterior would ever be deliberately altered so as to destroy its historic (i.e., charming) character are pretty small; the easement's value is, accordingly, much less than in the first case. And more important, if you are the owner of a unit in this building, the tax advantages of all unit-owners making

such a coordinated preservation easement donation, are likely
to far transcend any loss in value, if any, you may have to
contend with when you sell your unit.

Tax Benefits of Preservation Easements

What then are the tax advantages we're talking about
that are so magnificent it makes checking into such mushy
matters worthwhile? Let's return to the condo unit example
above. If it's a typical case of its kind, a qualified appraiser
is likely to find that the value of the donated easement would
equal roughly ten percent of each owner's unit. Now suppose
you owned one, and its fair market value is $75,000. The
value of your donation—which is treated for tax purposes
just like a charitable contribution—is $7,500. You are thus
able in the year of your donation, to deduct from your adjusted gross income for that year, $7,500. If you are in the
40 percent marginal tax bracket, you have saved $3,000 in
taxes! Like certain other charitable contributions, there is
a ceiling on how much you can deduct, equal to 30 percent
of your adjusted gross income that year (see Chapter 7). But
should you come up against that ceiling, don't fret—you can
carry the balance of the deduction forward—apply it to taxes
in future years—for up to five years.

Which Properties Qualify?

Generally speaking, a property will qualify if it: (1) is
listed individually in the National Register of Historic Places,
or (2) lies within a designated historic district which itself
is listed in the National Register; *and* is a certified historic
structure as described in Chapter 9, or (3) *perhaps*, if it fits
in neither of the above categories, but nonetheless is "significant to the visual or cultural heritage" of the locale in which
it is situated.

Now don't bank on your lovable little would-be landmark
being listed individually in the Register. Only about 27,000
properties are nationwide, and if yours is one of them you'd

know about it by now, by the number of preservation groups and other civic interests expressing interest in its future. Far more likely is the possibility that it lies within a part of town which local authorities have labelled an historic district, and have had their designation seconded by federal authorities (hence the district's listing in the Register). Many thousands of such buildings currently lie within such districts, and the number of districts is growing daily.

If you own a property you suspect may qualify, the first step is to contact local historic-preservation authorities to determine whether your hunch is right. If it is, get in touch with the people at L'Enfant Trust (write L'Enfant Trust, Christian Heurich Mansion, 1307 New Hampshire Avenue, N.W., Washington, D.C. 20036). They can send you a sample preservation easement deed which they've developed, and can help you obtain an architectural historian to prepare your certification application and find a licensed appraiser to determine the value of the easement you're donating.

Applying the Easement To Property You Don't Yet Own

Now suppose, Tom and Tammy Taxpayer, that you're like most Americans, and not only don't own a property that qualifies, but don't own *any* real estate at all. Just the same, you're tentatively in the market for a home to buy, and have decided you belong to that endangered species called the "Urban Dweller." Here is a prime opportunity to translate a bit of forward-thinking into a big chunk of the downpayment for that home.

What you need to do is very, very simple. First, make a list of the neighborhoods in your town that you would consider living in. Second, take that list to a local historic preservation group, and cross-check it against a list of certified historic districts in your town. The neighborhoods that make *both* lists are the ones in which you will concentrate your search. Third, take the winnowed-down new list around to several real-estate agents, and have them prepare a list of homes for sale in those neighborhoods in a price range you can afford (see Chapter 4). Fourth, go look at those places, and keep those on the list that you like.

Now you have yourself a list of candidate-homes that are *also potential* candidates for an historic preservation-easement donation. Fifth, through L'Enfant Trust or a group the Trust identifies, determine: (a) whether the particular buildings you're interested in would qualify for such a donation; (b) whether their current (or some prior) owner has already made one; and if not, (c) what such a donation would likely be worth.

Let's say you've performed all the above steps and come up with the perfect candidate: the owner is asking a price of $70,000, its fair market value, with a 10 percent downpayment, or $7,000. You've determined that a preservation easement donated on the property would be appraised at about 10 percent of its value, or $7,000, and you are in the 35 percent marginal tax bracket.

For a little extra work, you've constructed a situation enabling you potentially to cut the cost of your downpayment by 35 percent. You lay out the full $7,000 downpayment, of course—but just as quickly, once taking ownership of the property, you complete the donation of the easement. Your tax savings amounts to $7,000 × .35 = $2,450.

The Basis Reduction Rule Strikes Again

Whether the preservation-easement deduction you claim applies to a personal residence or a piece of investment, income-producing property, there is one slight drawback you need to be aware of, and it is, once again, the "basis reduction rule." Recall from Chapter 4 that the "basis" of your property is a measure used to calculate your taxable profits upon sale. When capital improvements are made, their cost is added to the property's basis—it is "adjusted upward"—and the taxable profits upon sale are reduced accordingly. Alternatively, depreciation taken on the property reduces the basis, causing correspondingly greater tax liability upon sale. When a preservation easement is donated, the basis of the affected property must be *reduced* by the value of the easement; hence, if the basis of your building (home or income property) is $60,000, and your easement donation is appraised at $6,000, your basis after donation will be adjusted downward to $54,000. Should you then sell the property for $65,000, you will owe tax (assuming for simplicity sake that no other tax-sheltering devices apply) on "profits" of $65,000 − $54,000 = $11,000.

But again, don't let this analysis leave you with the mistaken impression that *the entire* value of your easement donation will be recaptured sooner or later in taxes—that is, that this taxsaving device *only* accomplishes *deferral* of taxes owed. In reality it does much more—because the "profits" you will show upon sale, again assuming they are not otherwise sheltered, will be taxed at highly preferred, *capital gains* rates. Hence, your preservation-easement donation is not just a *deferral*-type tax shelter, but a *conversion*-type one as well, because the donation at the time you make it will be applied against the taxes you then owe at *ordinary-income rates*. Accordingly, to return to the example above: if you are in the 35 percent marginal tax bracket, then your $6,000 easement donation will be worth .35 × $6,000 = $2,100 to you in taxes saved at the time you make it. And when you sell the property (once more with the worst-case assumption that you can't shelter the profits), the additional taxes you'll owe because of the easement donation will be only $6,000 × .35 × .4 (preferred capital gains rate) = $840. You *still* come out $2,100 − $840 = $1,260 ahead, not counting any interest-income you were able to earn on the $2,100 during its deferral from taxation.

If it all sounds like alot of work—it really isn't, considering the rather substantial tax rewards that await you at the other end. And consider also that, again in the words of L'Enfant Trust, a preservation easement is a "gift to the street, and to the future—preserving the historical, social and architectural flavor of the neighborhood and its visual integrity for all to enjoy."

11

Preparing for Little
Tommy's College
Education

Little Tommy is only ten now. But he's outgrowing his
clothes faster than you can say "charge it," and just yester-
day he climbed up into your lap and cooed, as only the cutest
of sons can:

"Daddy, I want to go the the best college in the world
and learn about *everything,* just like you."

That sent Tammy scrambling for the Yale application
forms, so proud was she that her one-and-only could be so
forward-looking at so tender an age. But it hit you like a ton
of bricks, as you realized that in less than eight years Little
Tom will embark on an education adventure that could easily
set you back $40,000 or more. You ponder the sad fact that
your savings account has been growing so slowly of late, that
only a miracle would bring anything but a full-scholarship-
supported university education within your son's grasp.

Were Tommy old enough to be reading the newspapers,
he would know that the President of the United States—his
President—had proposed putting subsidized Guaranteed Student Loans, which helped get you through college, potentially
out of reach for families which like Tommy's earn more than
$30,000 a year. You would like to explain to him why Presi-
dent Reagan's budget recommendations for Fiscal Year 1983,
called for cutting combined federal spending for basic grants,
guaranteed loans and campus-based assistance, from the $6.7
billion spent in FY '81 to $6.0 billion in FY '83, to $3.8 billion
in FY '85. If only Tommy could comprehend that payments
to students under Social Security and the GI bill would drop

under the Administration's proposals from $4.1 billion in FY
'81 to just $700 million in FY '85.*

But you don't understand it, so why try to sell a ten-
year old kid? What looks to be an eight year-long panic sets
in. What *can* you do?

For starters, set Tommy's tiny mind at ease by telling
him that starting this very day, you will begin putting two
dollars and seventy-five cents away, *every* day for his education. And tell him that by performing this remarkably human
feat, you will have set aside a big chunk of what you figure
it will cost to send him through school, by the day he begins
college. That's just one of several things the tax code can
help you do to prepare for Little Tommy's college education.

In fact, you can *give* Tommy money, *loan* him money,
set up a *trust* for his benefit or even give him an *oil well*.
In each case, education-cutting Uncle Sam will be behind you
all the way.

Custodian Accounts

By setting $2.75 a day aside for Tommy, every day, you
will be able to fund a *custodian account* for your son at the
rate of $1,000 per year. This is the simplest mechanism for
saving money for Tommy with the tax system on our side.
Under the Uniform Gift to Minors Act, you, Tommy's
parents, can give him a *gift* of money or securities and let
the money he earns in interest or capital gains be taxed at
his tax rate, not yours.

What is the significance of the term "custodian account?" It means, simply, that when the account is opened
a custodian is named to manage its contents in the best interest of the minor, here your son Tommy. The custodian
so named may be your banker or your lawyer or your accountant, or a relative. It can even be either of you, Tommy's
parents—although if it is you, and you die before Tommy

* See June A. O'Neill and Margaret C. Simms, "Education," in *The
Reagan Experiment*, John L. Palmer and Isabel V. Sawhill, Eds.,
Washington, D.C., The Urban Institute Press, P. 352.

attains the age of majority, then the funds in the account will be included in your estate. It doesn't matter otherwise for tax purposes; the interest earned is still taxable to Little Tommy at Little Tommy's little rates. However, if the custodian allows the funds in the account to be used for any of Tommy's needs, then the funds so used will be taxed to the person—custodian or not—who bears the "legal obligation" to tend to those needs. (Local laws differ considerably on what needs it is a parent or guardian's "legal obligation" to provide. In this case, the ultimate goal is to save money for Tommy to devote to his education when he is no longer a minor, so the "legal obligation" trap shouldn't be a problem.)

Different states have differing rules as to when the funds in a custodian account must be distributed to the minor. Some say at age 18, others at age 21; but in either event, automatic distribution rules apply when Tommy reaches the age of majority as set by his state.

How The Custodian Account Works

Creating such a custodian account is usually a simpler feat then its alternative, creating a trust in Tommy's name. Trusts used to be the only way, until state-enacted Uniform Gifts to Minors Acts swept the nation.

Don't misunderstand: the $2.75 you'd be putting into Tommy's account every day comes from your *after*-tax income—it's in no way tax-exempt to you. But then, the money you'd some day be paying the lad's tuition bills with otherwise would be after-tax dollars too, so you may as well start letting the difference between his income tax rate and yours work for the both of you *right now*.

For simplicity's sake, let's assume Tommy matures into a worthless lout of an adolescent, who earns no money but the ten percent annual interest on the custodian account that has been set up for him. Presently, a dependent's first $1,000 of "unearned income" each year is tax free. From the

first deposit in Year One until withdrawal at the end of Year
Eight, the figures look something like this:

End of Year	Total on Deposit	Interest Earned*	Tax Paid**	Total
1	$1,000	$100	-0-	$1,100
2	$2,100	$210	-0-	$2,310
3	$3,310	$331	-0-	$3,641
4	$4,641	$464	-0-	$5,105
5	$6,105	$611	-0-	$6,716
6	$7,716	$772	-0-	$8,488
7	$9,488	$949	-0-	$10,437
8	$11,437	$1,144	$15.84	$12,565

* Actual interest earned will be somewhat less, especially in early years, due to the fact that
the deposits come in over the course of the year and not in a first-of-the-year lump sum.
** Taxes are zero in Years 1-7 because interest never exceeds $1,000; in Year 8 the excess
above $1,000 is assumed taxed at today's lowest, 11 percent rate.

Tommy's money is permitted to grow for him virtually
tax-free. Now what if you, instead of Tommy, had saved for
his education? Present law allows the exclusion from tax of
the first $100 in certain "qualified" dividends ($200 on a joint
return), but that exclusion doesn't extend to bank account
interest. Accordingly, all of that interest would be subject
to your full, 40 percent marginal income tax rate and the
eight-year results would be roughly as follows:

End of Year	Total on Deposit	Interest Earned	Tax Paid	New Total
1	$1,000	$100	$40	$1,060
2	$2,060	$206	$82	$2,184
3	$3,184	$318	$127	$3,375
4	$4,375	$438	$175	$4,638
5	$5,638	$564	$226	$5,976
6	$6,976	$698	$279	$7,395
7	$8,395	$840	$336	$8,899
8	$9,899	$990	$396	$10,493

Not only have you paid a total of $1,641 in federal income taxes you didn't really have to pay—a tragedy unto itself—you have also forfeited an additional $427 in interest that money could have earned for Tommy's education had it not been taxed away first.

Non-Cash Contributions

Custodian accounts can be funded with money. They can also be funded with stocks or bonds. Say, for instance, that Grandpa Taxpayer wants to give Tommy ten shares of Explosive Growth, Inc. stock for his birthday. Grandpa paid $5 a share for the stock; today it's worth $25. Grandpa, being in a 40 percent marginal tax bracket, would have to pay any capital gains tax on the sale at his rates In contrast, if he gives it to "X, as custodian for Tommy," Tommy's custodian has two choices. He can sell the stock; in that case, there would still be taxable "profit" upon sale, equal to the difference between the sales price ($25) and the purchase price ($5). But it would be taxed at *Tommy's* capital gains rate rather than Grandpa's, leading to considerable (if not total) savings of tax on those profits. The second thing Tommy's custodian might do is keep the stock, letting it earn income in the form of dividends. Those dividends would be taxed as ordinary income to Tommy, but again, at Tommy's rates.

There is absolutely no limit on the size of contributions to a custodian account, or their source or their frequency. You (or anyone else) can add to it as regularly or irregularly as you'd like. But all contributions to it are *gifts*. They belong to Tommy, and are at his completely discretionary disposal once he makes it to majority.

The Clifford Trust Alternative

Now suppose you want Tommy to be able to save for college with the savings being taxed at his rates, not yours—but at the same time, you just don't want to *give* him that much money. (For all you know, the kid could turn 21 and blow it all on a trip around the world.) So you turn to the second device, known in the trade as a *Clifford Trust*.

The central feature of a Clifford Trust is its *irrevocability*. You, as the "grantor," place assets (cash, stocks, property) into the trust for a term of *at least ten years plus one day;* during that time those assets (the trust "corpus") cannot be fiddled with by you. During the term of the trust, the individual or institution-appointed "trustee" manages the trust in the best interests of Tommy (the "beneficiary"), paying out to Tommy—or his custodian—the amount of income the trust earns every year. That income is taxed to Tommy, at Tommy's rates; it can be spent, saved or even placed in a custodian account created to receive it. After ten years plus one day, the "corpus" of the trust "reverts" to the grantor—you.

Interest-Free Loan

But suppose you just aren't sure you can afford to tie up all that much money for ten years plus one day. What to do? You use the third device, *an interest-free demand loan.* These loans are commonly called "Crown loans" for the gentleman who led the way by giving many millions in loans to each of his several children.

Here's a simple, one-shot example of how a Crown loan works. You loan Tommy $1,000 this year. You draw up a written agreement with your son which makes clear that no interest will be charged on the loan, but that repayment can *be demanded* at any time. (Tommy, being a minor, will of course have to have the document signed by his legal guardian, in this case probably your spouse.)

The loan proceeds would then be invested in the highest-yield savings certificate, bond or other instrument you can find. The interest is taxed, of course, but at Tommy's rates, not yours. And then, at some future time—whenever you need the money, or when Tommy enters school—you demand back the principal.

Tax-free loans are to the taxman what red capes represent to a taunted bull: he regularly races after them, and just as regularly gets zapped right between the horns. Tax attorneys familiar with the device say that taxpayers will likely continue to prevail against IRS, provided the loan-instrument evidences a clear intention that the loan *is* a debt that has to be repaid upon demand, and that the loan isn't forgiven (in which case it becomes a gift, and might be subject to the gift tax—see Page 143). The odds are, therefore, that if you try it you'll like it.

Putting Tommy In The Oil Business

There's still another way to get a nice chunk of Little Tommy's education bill behind you with some hefty help from Uncle Sam. It's somewhat risky, and it works only if you're in at least the 40-45 percent bracket in tax years '83 and beyond. You'll especially like this if you're a fan of the *Dallas* TV show and think of Little Tommy as the "John Ross Ewing" in your life .... because Tommy's going into the oil business.

As explained by James D. Whelan, a Washington, D.C. account executive with the the Dean Witter Reynolds, Inc. securities firm, here is how you, by buying into a typical oil and gas-drilling tax shelter, can help Tommy get his education.

Threshold assumption: You have $10,000 cash to invest today, knowing with a substantial degree of certainty that over the next two years, about 50 cents of every dollar will come back to you in the form of taxes saved if you're in the 45+ percent bracket. If that assumption fits you, read on:

• *Step One:* Locate an accountant, stockbroker or other investment counselor with a solid background in tax shelters generally, and "oil and gas limited partnerships" specifically. Ask for references and check them out: if his investment advice has proved responsible in the past, and if he can demonstrate that his firm has the resources to properly

evaluate and select the best of the hundreds of such shelters
on the market, move to Step Two.

• *Step Two:* Identify an "oil and gas limited partnership" that seems like the best bet for you. Stop right there:
what is an "oil and gas limited partnership"?

What's An Oil And Gas Limited Partnership

An oil and gas limited partnership is an increasingly
popular method used by those in the business of exploring
for oil here in the United States, to attract investors outside the business who'll put up most of the money it takes
to lease land to drill on, and pay drilling costs. The fellow
in the oil business—he may be a single individual, or a large
corporation—is called the "general partner," and his share
of the partnership in the venture you undertake with him
is usually based not on funds he invests, but on the time and
technical expertise he brings and devotes to the project.

Most commonly, this general partner will contract with
a stockbroker or other investment advisor to offer shares
in a planned drilling program to the public; these shares are
sold as "units," typically for $5,000 or $10,000 apiece. Those
who buy them are called the "limited partners," a legal term
with two important meanings you need to know. The first
is that the term "limited" means your liability, in the event
the venture fails to make money or break even, is "limited"
to the extent of your contracted-upon investment—in this
case the price of your units. The second meaning of the term
is that your involvement in the project is "limited" to the
status of silent investor: you have no say in the day-to-day
management of the operation.

Despite your "limited" status, *you* are nevertheless a
partner in the venture, and that fact alone carries one extremely important tax consequence: any tax benefits that
accrue to the partnership, *pass through it* directly to you,
the partners. Unlike a corporation, which pays taxes and
takes its own tax-breaks instead of passing them on to
shareholders, a partnership is not a "taxable entity" under

the law; so if it earns investment credits or depreciation deductions or other tax benefits, you, the partners, get to apply them against your own individual federal income tax liability in the year they accrue to the partnership.

So much for the term "limited partnership." There are as many purposes for limited partnerships today as there are investment ideas. Real estate investment, equipment-leasing and oil-and-gas exploration are perhaps the most common varieties, but of late partnerships have sprung up to invest in other areas particularly favored under the new tax laws, such as research and development. But what you're looking for here, because of its peculiar tax and investment return characteristics, is a limited partnership in the oil and gas biz.

Exploratory, Developmental And Hybrid Partnerships

There are three basic varieties of oil-and-gas drilling tax shelters (we'll get to why these limited partnerships are also "tax shelters" in a minute). First, there are those involved primarily in *exploratory* oil and gas drilling—set up to explore land areas which are so far unproved as to their potential. Second, there are partnerships involved primarily in *developmental* drilling—concentrating on lands that are more promising because oil and/or gas have already been discovered nearby.

Quite obviously, the risk of turning up "dry holes" in an exploratory venture is considerably greater than in a developmental one. But at the same time, because unproven lands can be quite a bit cheaper to lease for drilling than already tried-and-true ones, the exploratory venture may be able to drill more holes in more places than the developmental venture, for the same cost.

The third form of partnership—and the one you'll see is best suited to Tommy's schooling needs—is really a hybrid of the other two. In its case, the money raised from silent, limited-partner investors will be used by the general partners to drill exploratory *and* developmental wells in some pre-determined ratio, say 50-50, or two "conservative" developmental holes to one "high risk" exploratory one, etc.

What we are trying to find in Step Two is, believe it or not, a balanced drilling program that is likely to prove "averagely successful." That's because the averagely successful partnership will return to the limited partner roughly twice his original investment, *exclusive of tax benefits*, over roughly a ten-year period following the year of investment.

A major caveat you must heed at this point: there is absolutely no guarantee whatsoever that *any* of the wells drilled by your particular partnership will be successful. In that event, you will lose your entire investment, less the tax savings you will gain by making the investment in the first place. But of course it's also possible that your partnership will do a bit better than or well beyond the average, and returns of 6-to-1 and higher are not unheard of.

• *Step Three:* Your advisor has found the partnership that seems to fit the bill. Its units sell for $5,000 apiece, with a minimum purchase of two units ($10,000) required. A second major caveat you must now recognize: those units are *not* shares in a major company which can be readily traded on a public stock exchange. They are what financial people call a relatively "illiquid" investment, in that although you *may* be presented with one or more opportunities to "liquidate" (sell) your units or exchange them at some later time for publicly traded stock, you should assume at the time you buy them that you will *not* be able to sell out for cash in the event you suddenly need that money. Aware of that caveat, you decide you can afford to tie up your funds, and you plunk down the ten grand.

• *Step Four:* You take the *tax advantages* of your investment. We said oil-and-gas drilling partnerships are a "tax shelter" and that they truly are, because of the important tax deductions available for minerals exploration that can be passed on to you. These involve primarily "intangible drilling costs" associated with the exploration phase of the venture, and in a typical partnership these costs are substantial enough to permit you, the partner, *a deduction equal to virtually 100 percent of your $10,000 investment* spread over years one and two of your involvement in the partnership.

Note very carefully what this means. Had you bought your units at the outset of 1983, for $10,000, and your partnership has been carefully selected, you would be eligible for a deduction in tax year 1983 of about $7—9,000; and a deduction for the balance—$3—$1,000—in tax year 1984. Now if you'll be in the 40 percent marginal tax bracket in 1983, and your deduction in that year is, say, $7,000, you will save .4 × $7,000 = $2,800 in taxes, reducing *your* funds actually still at risk in the partnership to $10,000 − $2,800 = $7,200. And in 1984, you'll take an additional $3,000 deduction, saving another .4 × $3,000 = $1,200 in taxes, and further lowering your funds still at risk to $7,200 − $1,200 = 6,000.*

Looking at the situation another way: by the end of the 1984 tax year, your involvement in the oil and gas partnership will be $6,000, and Uncle Sam's will be $4,000—although *you alone still* own those two units, and are *still* anticipating that average two-to-one return *on your original $10,000 investment.*

• *Step Five:* You're now in the third year of owning the partnership, and this is usually the time when the general partner will report to you on the success (or failure) of your drilling program. You will receive an evaluation of your two units; and typically, if the programs's success is average, that evaluation will come in at between $3,500—$7,500 for those two units. A figure in between would suggest that you can expect your "payout" over the next seven years—your share of the value of the oil and gas that's been discovered, pumped and sold during that time—to come to roughly twice your original ten grand, or $20,000.

---

* To assume that your tax bracket remains relatively constant between 1983 and 1984, given the Administration tax cuts enacted in 1981, further assumes that your income will rise between those years. This is not an unreasonable assumption to make, given predictions of an improving economy and continuing noises about a possible cutback in the cuts themselves.

• *Step Six:* Turn to Tommy, who's just celebrated his thirteenth birthday. With great fanfare, give him the birthday present of his life: the certificate of ownership to those two units of the partnership. To use that strange verb that tax experts invented to describe the glorious event: "gift" your interest in the partnership to your son.

Why? Because *you* got what you wanted out of the deal: $4,000 in tax savings. And now it's time for Tommy to get what *you* want *him* to get out of the deal: $20,000 in tuition money, taxed at Tommy's little tax rate, spread over the next seven years, *at a total cost to you of only $6,000.* You can generally expect those income payments to come in amounts approximating a bell curve on a graph: slowly at first, rising to a maximum and then dipping again.

Tommy will have three tax advantages of his own. First, about 15 percent of his income from partnership payments will be offset by a deduction known as the oil depletion allowance, which the partnership gets and passes on to Tommy, who is now the limited partner. Second, Tommy will be taxed at *his* income rate, which is considerably lower than yours. And third, because the return is spread out over roughly seven years instead of paid in one lump sum, the rate of tax paid on it is even smaller.

There are variations on this plan you can explore with your accountant, lawyer or banker. Perhaps, instead of giving the units to Tommy outright, it would be preferable to place them in a trust for your son, with release of the units and accumulated income to him on the day he reaches the age of majority or begins college. Of course, you can keep the units and take some of that income yourself (at your 40 percent rate!), "gifting" what's left to your son at any later date.

The point is, Uncle Sam is going to great lengths to (a) permit you to help develop the country's domestic fossil-fuel base at a good profit to yourself, and (b) provide for your son's education. Don't scorn him—go for it.

The Gift Tax

A word about the gift tax. Really a word or two is all it's worth, because its bark is much, much worse than its bite.

Here are the major features of the gift tax that, as you can see, make it highly unlikely that the tax will play a role in your financial affairs:

• The tax applies only to *non*-tax-deductible gifts. When the gift we're talking about is a deductible *charitable* contribution (see Chapter 7), the tax doesn't even come into play.

• Where non-deductible contributions are involved, you may make gifts of *up to $10,000 to each* of as many different individuals or organizations you want, *each year* without triggering any gift-tax liability. For married couples, the ceiling rises to $20,000. Taking Little Tommy as an example, you and Tammy may "gift" him up to $20,000 *every year* without worrying about owing gift taxes.

• Any amount *beyond* your $10,000 ($20,000 if married) ceiling is subject to gift tax *only if the amount above the ceiling takes you beyond the limit of your lifetime exemption.*. The "lifetime exemption" is the amount, beyond the per-recipient annual limitations, which you can contribute over the course of your lifetime without incurring gift tax liability. This lifetime exemption is pretty high—and rising. Here is where it would presently stand for the years 1982—1987:

1982	$225,000
1983	$275,000
1984	$325,000
1985	$400,000
1986	$500,000
1987	$600,000

(Source: *The Gift Giving Guide*, P. 19.)

Here's what those lifetime exemptions mean: In 1984, the only possible way in which you would be subject to gift-tax under current law would be if you give Little Tommy more than $20,000 that year, *and* your non-deductible gifts to all recipients *above the annual per-recipient exclusion,* during the course of your own lifetime up to and including 1984, exceed $325,000.

One cautionary note: to keep things simple we have not explained, up to this point, that the lifetime exemption also applies to the taxes your *estate* could owe upon your death. For instance, should you die in 1985, having made $300,000 in beyond-the-annual-exclusion gifts, then $100,000 of your total $400,000 life exemption (as it will stand in 1985) will be left to apply against your estate tax liability, whatever that will be.

In practice, Tom and Tammy, the gift tax is today of concern only when pretty sizable transfers of money or other assets, or large estates, are involved. And when it does apply it is taxable to the giver, not the recipient, so Little Tommy doesn't need to worry about it either. But do keep your eye on Congress, just in case it gets it into its collective head that toughening up on the gift tax's virtual non-applicability to little people would somehow be good for the country.

12

Live In Sin
A While Longer

About 1.2 million divorces in the U.S. were granted in 1981. That's a rate of just under one divorce for every 2 marriages—and its *triple* the divorce rate of 20 years ago. Clearly, Americans everywhere are taking "till death do us part" a little less to heart than before. But could our high-minded, mightily moral tax system be playing a role?

Few quirks in the tax law have gotten as much attention of late as the so-called "marriage penalty." The issue is simply this: when a man and woman marry, and both are wage-earners, they will be taxed on their "combined income" at a higher rate than each would be taxed on his or her income alone. Her is how the "marriage penalty" worked in tax year 1981.

Let's say Tom Taxpayer had taxable income of $28,000 that year, and his fiancee, Tammy Tucker (soon to become Tammy Taxpayer, we know) had taxable income of $10,800. Under the tax rates in effect that year, Tom, filing singly, would have paid $7,043 in federal income taxes, and Tammy would have paid $1,541 for a total of $8,584. Now suppose instead that Tom and Tammy married *anytime* during 1981. Their combined taxable income would then have been $28,800 + 10,800 = $39,600. Had they paid their taxes as married persons filing separate returns their total would have been $10,577, a whopping $1,993 higher than what they owed as singles. Had they filed a joint return, they would have owed $9,939, still $1,355 more than under their single status. Hence the term "marriage penalty": more than one couple came to realize that their honeymoon was truly over come April 15.

It wasn't long before some of the more irate marriage penalty-payers struck upon the device of divorcing in late December and re-marrying in early January, while using the money they saved in taxes to pay for a quickie Tijuana divorce and Acapulco honeymoon.

The taxman was not amused: the IRS issued a revenue ruling in 1976, noting with a sniff of its administrative nose that "The tax law does not contemplate a sham transaction that manipulates year-end marital status for federal income tax purposes."

Recently, having been made aware that many constituents are married persons, Congress sprang into action. In 1982 there was, for the first time, a marriage penalty tax-deduction for married two-earner couples that partially offset, but did not eliminate, the penalty. For 1983, the deduction works as follows: whichever of the two-earner couple earns the lesser amount, will be permitted to deduct ten percent of his or her "qualified earned income," up to a maximum income-level of $30,000. "Qualified earned income" means income derived from such sources as wages, fees, commissions and the like, as opposed to income that money "earns," such as dividends and interest, which are not included in the definition. Also excluded would be unemployment compensation, salary paid by one spouse to the other, and deferred retirement income like pension annuities or Individual Retirement Account (IRA) disbursements. The $30,000 ceiling coupled with 1983's ten-percent deduction means that this year, the lesser-earning spouse who earns $30,000 of qualified earned income or more may deduct $3,000 from her taxable income. Still, the "marriage penalty" to some extent remains.

So much for that well-known quirk—perhaps it says something about our society that the tax code should enter adversely into one's decision whether or not to marry. But there's another, lesser-known quirk that's even stranger, to wit: believe it or not, Uncle Sam *appreciates divorces!*

What? You're kidding! Show me where on the tax form it says that divorces are a good thing, you demand. No kidding, it's there. But not to the naked eye—you need a sharp divorce lawyer to see it with crystal clarity, and most of us don't go to a divorce lawyer for help with our taxes. So please don't consider what follows as "tax advice;" just file it away as a great cocktail-party conversation-piece, and do whatever you do with it without telling anybody where you got it. Thank you. Now here it is:

Suppose, Tom and Tammy, that you're married, and that your annual household expenses for food, rent, medical expenses and so on, come to $25,000. Let's say for the sake of this illustration that those expenses divide up evenly between you, at $12,500 apiece. As a married couple your combined $39,600 taxable income would place you in the 35 percent marginal tax bracket in 1983. As singles, however, Tom's bracket would be around 36 percent, and Tammy's would be around 17 percent, a big difference.

Now as you already know, those general household expenses we listed above are not under ordinary circumstances tax-deductible; you have to pay for them in after-tax dollars. No surprises there. But suppose you and Tammy have a horrible fight . . . . irreconcilable differences present themselves . . . . Tom moves into a hotel room and Tammy hires a lawyer to draft a written separation agreement and file for divorce as soon as humanly possible. Her lawyer calls your lawyer and demands *"alimony"* and *"separate maintenance"* in the amount of $12,500 a year forever or until Tammy re-marries, whichever comes first.

Now watch what happens. If a written separation agreement is in effect, and/or a divorce decree is rendered, and if the payments Tammy demands fit into the proper legal definition of "alimony" or "separate support"—as all her household expenses listed above do—then that monthly payment is *deductible* from your gross income, and *includable* in hers.

Let's quickly work through the figures. Tom, your taxable income drops from $28,800 to $16,300, taxed at single-taxpayer rates, and your 1983 tax bill will be an estimated $2,400. Tammy's income rises from $10,800 to $23,300, and her tax bill will be around $4,300. The difference between your combined tax bills as divorcees —$6,700—and your estimated bill as marrieds—$7,800—is $1,100. Now, some of that amount is attributable to your new single status, i.e., getting out from under what's left of the marriage penalty. But the rest, is due to your sudden ability to transfer $12,500 worth of income to your *former* wife. Strange but true.

Everybody wants to save a buck, especially a thousand bucks a year, but isn't leaving Tammy going a little overboard, Tom is asking? The answer is as follows:

Does the law of the United States say that divorced or separated people must live apart? No. Does it say that they must not be on speaking, or lovemaking, terms with one another? Nope. Is there any clause in the laws which states that a man can't enjoy the fruits of a household which he is helping, through alimony and maintenance payments, to support? And if a couple divorced but continued to live happily together thereafter for the rest of their lives, would the taxman cometh forth with a ruling that such was "a sham transaction . . . . for tax purposes," and taketh you to court? Perhaps he'd try. But he'd have one heck of a fight on his hands . . . . and like we said, this one is for cocktail parties . . . .

13

The TADPOLE Tactic

"We at Acme Air Conditioning hope that this small amount of $35 will help you and our great country. All of the employees at Acme feel this way."

"Please accept this small gift of $40 I enclosed for the Federal Government of the United States of America. I feel that the Government can use all the help it can get."

"Dear Mr. President:
I am glad that you are our President. We hope you have a good year in 1973. Are you having a good time in Washington, D.C.? The $1 is to help you balance the budget."

Lest you wake up some mornings despondent that the American Spirit has withered away, these letters—and thousands of others like them from senders of all ages, from all reaches of the nation—are pretty powerful evidence that it is alive and kicking. Since somebody began keeping track in 1862, Uncle Sam has received more than $50 million in donations—from an anonymous seven-cent gift, to a $200,000 bequest from Oliver Wendell Holmes; from people who believe that when it comes to charitable giving, the country itself is pretty high on their list. Their gifts arrive with a multitude of explanations: to help balance the national debt; to express gratitude for American citizenship; to help maintain a public park that has given years of joy. Some just carry a note marked "Thank you."

This isn't a book about how to give more money to Uncle Sam than you have to—quite the opposite in fact. But if you're one out of every four Americans who identify

themselves as left-of-center politically . . . . if you believe that
the Federal Government can and should play an important
role in shaping social welfare programs . . . . then you've *got*
to be asking yourself: just how far am *I* willing to go in reducing *my* taxes, knowing that so many of the social programs *I* fought for, and still believe in, could suffer thereby?

Despite the recent Reagan cutbacks many of our programs still exist. ACTION is still around; low-income housing programs, Food Stamps, the Legal Services Corporation,
Medicare, non-military foreign aid—some may be faint
shadows of what they once were or what we'd like them to
be, but they continue to function and none of us, by launch-
ing a purported "Progressive Taxpayers' Revolt," want to
tantalize the President into wiping them out altogether in
a grand gesture of incumbent indignation.

Don't let your conscience scare you away—not yet. Read
on, for between the lines of those sweet one-dollar donations
to fend off the deficit, lies the germ of the greatest unused
political weapon of our time. You are about to learn:

* How to tell Ronald Reagan how you want your money
spent;

* How to, in effect, end-run the White House, OMB,
Pentagon and both appropriations committees of the Congress and impose *your* spending priorities on them;

* How to make the federal programs you hate *pay* for
your personal re-orientation of federal spending priorities;
and

* *How to save money* in the process.

This device is so special it deserves its own acronym:
the TADPOLE Tactic (for: Tax-Advantaged Donations to
Promote Ongoing Legitimate Expenditures). How does the
TADPOLE Tactic work? It's really very simple:

Once again, Tom and Tammy Taxpayer, let's suppose
you are an American household like many others. In tax year
1982, your joint taxable income was $25,000, and you paid
$4,160 in federal income taxes.

Now suppose that by using *any* of the legal tax-avoidance methods described in this book—it doesn't matter at all which one—you were able to reduce your *taxes owed* by $200. By that fact alone, you are $200 "richer" that you would have been otherwise. ("Richer" is in quotes because it does not necessarily follow that you now have $200 more cash-in-hand—"disposable income"—to spend; it may be tied up as equity in a particular tax-advantaged investment you selected. But no matter: your actual "net worth" has increased by $200, and that's what's key here.)

Now if your goal in making that tax-spawned investment decision was *purely financial*, fine. The analysis is over . . . . you have kept your hard-won cash out of Uncle Sam's clutches, and needn't concern yourself with anything more than tending your tax shelter to ensure that it ultimately disgorges your investment as designed.

But pure financial self-interest might not be your *sole* motivation. You may have decided to avoid *paying* federal income taxes as a way of making a statement against the manner in which the present Administration has elected to *spend* your tax dollars. You may be a fine, upstanding, patriotic American who counts it a fundamental attribute of civic duty to pay taxes . . . . for whom April 15 is no less a day to express one's patriotism and pride than the first Tuesday in any election-year November. But—and it's a *big* but—you can't stomach the thought of watching *your* salary subsidize a hardened missile silo somewhere in Wyoming, while some infant child of an unemployed autoworker is going to bed cold and hungry in Michigan. (Sounds strange? Just hark back to the days when young, patriotic Americans willing to die for their country, sought refuge instead in Canada, Sweden and anywhere rather than fight an aimless war in Southeast Asia. Conscientious-objector status has long been recognized in the warmaking arena—isn't it about time it applied to taxpaying too?)

So if you count yourself in this latter category, or even if your motivations are mixed, consider this: you *can*, while

avoiding taxes, selectively subsidize some of those federal
programs you believe in, *and save* money doing so.

You just do what the senior American Government class
at Milford High School did when it sent $6.42 in to the United
States Treasury "to help clear the national debt." *You donate
your tax savings (or some part of it) to Uncle Sam.*

Let's go back to that example of $200 in taxes saved
mentioned a bit ago. Suppose you truly believe that Social
Security is a good program; that it works well; that it effectively redistributes income from the able-bodied haves to the
elderly and disabled have-nots. So suppose you want to give
Social Security a little bit of extra help—so take, let's say,
$50 of that $200 tax savings and *donate* it to the Social
Security Administration. Send it in with the following note
(all rhetoric to be molded according to your own particular
style, of course.)

> The Honorable Donald T. Regan
> Secretary of the Treasury
> (As Acting Trustee, Social Security Trust Fund)
> Fifth Street and Pennsylvania Avenue, NW
> Washington, D.C. 20220
>
> Dear Secretary Regan:
>
> Enclosed please find my check for $50, made
> payable to the Social Security Trust Fund.
>
> This check represents my personal contribu-
> tion to the Social Security Trust Fund, and I would
> like to have it earmarked specifically for the Old
> Age and Survivors Insurance Fund. I believe that
> this program embodies the spirit of caring and shar-
> ing that sets us apart, as a nation, from any other
> in the western world. I would respectfully request
> you to spend this donation for and only for the
> Social Security program indicated, and to treat this
> sum as above and beyond any moneys proposed to

be spent by the President and/or authorized and appropriated by the U.S. Congress. Should this for any reason not prove possible, please return my check immediately.

Sincerely,

Tom Taxpayer and Family

Voila! In two revolutionary paragraphs you have accomplished the following:

• You have taken $50 that would, but for your new tax-saving discoveries, have been paid in federal income taxes—that is, into the general fund from whence most all federal progams are funded—and have allocated it instead to the federal program *of your choice*.

• *You—not* the President, *not* David Stockman, *not* some Pentagon analyst, *not* the House and Senate Appropriations Committees—have decided how that $50 shall be spent. That alone, Tom and Tammy, could be perhaps the single biggest leap toward true popular democracy this country has seen since one-person-one-vote.

• Note where that $50 has *come from.* To say that it has come from the pocket of Tom Taxpayer is true, but only partly true—since, after all, you were prepared before to blindly pay away that $50 in no-strings-attached taxes anyway. So it is really more accurate to say that this $50 has been rescued directly from the tax pool, the general fund. And what normally happens to money which goes into the general fund? It is allocated the way the President and Congress want it to be allocated: in Fiscal Year 1981, for instance, 24.3 cents of each federal budget dollar went into national defense. And in FY 1986, if the President has his way, that share will rise to 35.8 cents.*

---

* John L. Palmer and Gregory B. Mills, "Budget Policy," in *The Reagan Experiment*, P. 74. Figures for 1986 are from the Administration's FY 1983 budget proposals.

In sum, of the $50 you have just contributed to the program of your choice, Tom and Tammy, at least 24.3%, or $12.15, has been pulled right out of the hands of the generals. Magnifique, n'est pas?

• And here is what the French call the "coupe de grace"—the icing on the cake, so to speak. Not only have you *allocated* your money to your favorite program; you also get to claim a *tax deduction* for your contribution, just as if you had given it to your favorite charity! Being roughly in the 26 percent marginal tax bracket, you get to deduct .26 × $50 = $13 from your *next year's* federal income taxes. That $13 represents a whole new tax shelter to you, small as it is . . . . more tax savings, and a chance to start the same process all over again. And so—by saving $50 in taxes, and giving it back to the government as a donation, you are really "spending" only $37; you've "made" money spending Uncle Sam's money your way. Not bad, huh?

Of course this "savings" increases along with income level and tax brackets. Irony-lovers should note that for single taxpayers earning $42,000 or more—which in tax year 1981 would have placed them in a 55 percent marginal tax bracket—a gift to a particular hand-picked federal program of $100 would actually have cost the general fund $55, *more* than its cost *to that taxpayer*. In other words, the 50 percent, top-bracket taxpayer today not only has the luxury of selecting which programs to support—Uncle Sam will back her with matching funds!

Now a natural question presents itself: how do you, Tom Taxpayer, go about finding out whether the federal agency or program you want to selectively support would accept such a contribution, and if so, who to send it to?

The U.S. Treasury lists more than 40 separate accounts to which funds have been contributed in the past.*

* Department of the Treasury, Fiscal Service, *Combined Statement of Receipts, Expenditures and Balances of the United States Government for the Fiscal Year Ended September 30, 1981*, Pp. 32-33.

The table on the following pages gives name, address, and proper contact of several sample agencies or programs that are known to accept such contributions, along with any special instructions you need to know.

Progressive-minded taxpayers should be proud to invoke the TADPOLE Tactic. President Reagan ought to be too, in fact, for it encourages something in all of us he's called for time and time again: a greater spirit of private philanthropy to fill the great gap that "necessary" reductions in "social" programs have brought about—"a torrent of private initiatives that will astound the advocates of big government."

We'll try, Mr. President, we'll try.

AGENCY	NAME/ADDRESS	SPECIAL INSTRUCTIONS
ACTION	Tom Pauken, Director ACTION 806 Connecticut Avenue, NW Washington, DC 20525	Contributions are specifically authorized under Sec. 402(5) of the Domestic Volunteer Services Act of 1973 as amended. Can be in cash or in-kind.
National Park Sevice	Russell Dickenson, Director, National Park Service U.S. Department of the Interior 18th & C Streets, NW Washington, DC 20240	Can be general contributions, or specific as to purpose or location. Several national parks have published their own catalogues of gifts they would like to receive. Gifts can be in cash or in-kind.
U.S. Fish and Wildlife Service	Robert Jantzen, Director U.S. Fish and Wildlife Service U.S. Department of the Interior 18th & C Streets, NW Washington, DC 20240	Can be in cash or in-kind.
Legal Services Corporation	Donald P. Bogard, President Legal Services Corporation 733 15th Street, NW Washington, DC 20005	The Corporation is an independent, Congressionally-created entity classified under Sec. 501(c)(3) of the Internal Revenue Code (non-profit, tax-exempt charitable organization).
Department of Health and Human Sevices	Assistant Secretary for Management and Budget, U.S. Department of Health and Human Services 330 Independence Avenue, SW Washington, DC 20201	You might try to earmark your gift to a particular program; however it's uncertain whether the department will comply with your request.
Social Security Administration	Donald T. Regan Secretary of the Treasury (As Acting Trustee, Social Security Trust Fund) 15th & Pennsylvania Ave., NW Washington, DC 20220	Cash-only gifts may be directed to any of four Social Security Trust Funds: (1) Old Age and Survivors Insurance; (2) Disability Insurance; (3) Hospital Insurance and (4) Supplementary Medical Insurance. In the event no designation is made the gift is automatically put into the Old Age and Survivors Insurance Trust Fund.

AGENCY	NAME/ADDRESS	SPECIAL INSTRUCTIONS
General Funds ▲ Gifts to the United States	Bureau of Government Financial Operations Treasury Annex #1 Room 300, Madison Pl. and Pennsylvania Ave., NW Washington, DC 20226	Cash or in-kind gifts (which are sold at auction) accepted. All gifts go into the general fund.
▲ Conscience Fund	(SAME)	For those gifts sent by "guilty conscience" anonymous taxpayers who feel they underpaid in a prior year. Gifts go into the general fund.
▲ Gifts for Reduction of the Public Debt	(SAME)	For gifts whose donors specify reducing the debt, or deficit, as the purpose.
▲ National Defense Conditional Gift	(SAME)	For gifts whose donors specify the national defense as the purpose.

14 The Coming Tax Revolt

"Taxes are what we pay for a civilized society."
Justice Oliver Wendell Holmes, Jr.

"Taxation without representation is tyranny."
American Revolutionary James Otis

*"The mind-set of America has changed since World War
II... The concept of civil disobedience, of demonstrations
against authority, has people acting in a way that would not
have been considered patriotic or acceptable in the past... It
is not as antisocial as it was to evade taxes."*
Internal Revenue Service Commissioner
Roscoe Egger, Jr.*

It's Panic City out there.

"TAX CHEATING—Bad and Getting Worse" screams
the headline of the Time Magazine cover story, which goes
on to warn that tax evasion "is becoming not just a sickness
but an epidemic, no longer secret but widely admitted, even
joked about and accepted." "Where are They? Hidden
Billions," demands the *New York Daily News*. "Prying Open
the Underbelly Economy Reveals a Can of Worms," worries
the *Washington Post*. Even *Psychology Today* weighs in,
with "The Tax-Evasion Virus."
The U.S. General Accounting Office issues a report, in-
ocuously entitled, "Illegal Tax Protestors Threaten the Tax
System." The Internal Revenue Service forms its own tax-
rebel rat patrol, the "IRS Illegal Tax Protestor Program,"
and compiles a three-inch thick handbook on the subject for
its PR people filled with Dragnet-style tales of doctors, pilots,

* Quoted in "TAX CHEATING—Bad and Getting Worse," *Time
Magazine*, March 28, 1983, P.27

real estate agents and hundreds of other average joes who
tried to cheat and got squashed.*

A trade association of certified public accountants—a
profession not prone to emotional outbursts—is concerned
enough about the volume of cash traveling through the untaxed "underground economy" to officially recommend doing away with all currency larger than $50 bills—or at least
having them "expire periodically." Its 1983 study of the
problem concludes that voluntary compliance with the
Federal income tax system "has reached serious propor-
tions," and that if the situation continues to worsen, it could
lead to the disruption of our economy and even to a
breakdown in society if Congress finds itself unable to raise
sufficient revenue ... The so-called tax gap is enormous by
anyone's estimate and is growing larger," it says.**

The "tax gap"?

The "tax gap" is to the Treasury what the "generation
gap" was to parents of the 60's, the "credibility gap" was
to Nixon in the 70's, and the "gender gap" is to Reagan today. It can't be wished away; it is an uncomfortable, uncon-
trollable ulcer on the underside of the seat of power in the
western world.

The "tax gap" is officially defined as "the difference between the total amount of income tax which is voluntarily
paid for a given tax year, and the correct tax liability for
that year." In other words, the shortfall between what Uncle

---

* A sample gem:
"In *United States v. Alpan* ... Alpan, a dentist, was convicted for 3 counts
of failing to file returns for 1973 through 1975. Alpan became involved
with a leader of the tax protest movement, Lucille Moran who prevailed
upon him to create his individual church, the Liberal Church, and to refuse
to file his income tax returns. He transferred his home and rental properties to the church and the church transferred them to his wife. Alpan
received a one year prison sentence, 9 months suspended, and a $15,000
fine."

** "Underreported Taxable Income: The Problems and Possible Solu-
tions," American Institute of Certified Public Accountants, Washington,
D.C., 1983, Pp. 43, 5-6.

Sam *should* be collecting in income taxes for any given year, and what he *actually* collects. Ten years ago the total tax gap, according to IRS, was $30.9 billion. By 1981 it had tripled to $90.5 billion, and it is now projected to pass $120 billion by 1985, a hefty slice of the federal deficit Reaganomics will give us that year.

Maybe it *is* time for a little national panicking:

• In 1978, 5,694 American taxpayers filed "protest" returns—that is, tax returns which stated any grounds for refusing to pay less than what IRS thought was the right amount of taxes owed. In 1979 the number of "protest" returns passed 8,700; in 1980, it hit 10,587. In 1981 it nearly doubled to 20,962, and in 1982 it nearly doubled again to 39,569. If this growth rate continues, more than one million Americans will be filing "protest" returns by 1987.

• In a 1980 private survey for the IRS, those interviewed were asked to rank a list of crimes in order of seriousness—stealing $500 from an employer; illegally obtaining it in food stamps or welfare payments; stealing it from a giant corporation, or cheating Uncle Sam out of $500 in taxes. Most rated the tax cheat a pretty distant last. What's more, the higher the respondent's level of education, the less likely the tax-cheating offense was to be rated "very serious." And more than one out of four interviewees in the same survey admitted to failing to report some income on their *own* tax returns.*

• "Tax protesting" has become a profession unto itself. The prince of protesters is Irwin Schiff, a talk-showman with two bestselling books, a newsletter claiming over 4,000 subscribers, a booming seminar business and four months in jail (for willful failure to file a return) to his credit. Mr. Schiff says he's "stopped 300,000 persons from paying income taxes altogether," taking the increasingly popular position that under the Constitution and tax code as currently

* "A General Taxpayer Opinion Survey" prepared by CSR, Inc., for the Internal Revenue Service Office of Planning and Research, Washington, D.C., March 1980, pp. 67, 89.

written, taxpaying is a purely voluntary act. But he vehemently eschews the "protester" label, preferring to call himself an "educator."

• By far the largest component of the "tax gap"—some $50 billion says the IRS—is attributable not to overinflated deduction claims, false dependents and the like, but to income which is never reported. And much of that unreported income is the forbidden fruit of the so-called "underground economy."

The "Underground Economy"

In France they call it "travail au noir," meaning "black labor," and estimate that it involves some 800,000 workers and may account for 25 percent of the official economy—large enough to spur the French government into a media-and-poster blitz trumpeting the folly of hiring moonlighting plumbers, hairdressers and policemen. Italy's "l'economia submersa" is reported "growing so rapidly that the government now includes it in economic planning."* West German authorities in 1979 put the value of untaxed "Schwarzarbeit" at $25 billion, and claimed that one-fourth of the country's jobless could find work if it were eliminated. Great Britain's "fiddling" is now estimated at around 15 percent of its national output. And as bad as the problem is in western Europe—bad enough that the Organization for Economic Cooperation and Development has made studying it a priority—officials in Thailand guess that less than 10 percent of that country's 19 million workers even bother to file tax returns.**

So should *we* be complaining?

Just how big the U.S. underground economy is, nobody can say for sure: unofficial estimates for 1981 range from $250 billion to $800 billion, depending on just which expert you ask. But those experts do agree on one point—that the underground unreported-income economy is growing "two

*"Cheating on Taxes—A Worldwide Pursuit," *U.S. News & World Report*, Oct. 22, 1979, P. 53.
** "Cheating on Taxes," *U.S. News*, P. 56.

or three times faster than the regular enconomy,"* meaning that a steadily growing share of our Gross National Product will be slipping by the Taxman's nose.

The IRS has taken to separating the underground
economy into two "sectors," the "legal" and the "illegal."
The "legal" sector includes moonlighting nightwatchmen,
slippery landlords and tip-pocketing maitre-d's; that is, those
of us who earn our money lawfully, but just don't care to
pay taxes on it. In 1981, just under $250 billion in legal in-
come went untaxed. The "illegal" sector pertains to drug
dealers, gamblers and prostitutes who are not merely con-
tent to break the law by what they do but also tend to forget
to pay taxes, too. In 1981 $9 billion of illegal income went
untaxed, with over two-thirds attributed to illegal drug traf-
ficking. (One unfortunate soul recently tried arguing that being forced to disclose gambling income on his tax return
would amount to unconstitutionally compelled self-
incrimination. The court sent him scrambling, ruling that
the Fifth Amendment was intended to serve as a "shield"
against being forced to implicate oneself in a *prior* crime, not
as a "sword" enabling the commission of an *additional* crime
of tax evasion.)

What ought to have the government worried, though,
is the magnitude of the "legal" sector—specifically, the fact
that the percentage of legal income being voluntarily
reported is on a slow but steady decline. In 1981, more than
one out of every ten dollars in legally earned income were
never reported. And the biggest culprits by a mile were those
who earned "capital gains" income from the sale of stocks,
real estate and other assets: only 59.4 percent of capital gains
income was reported as it should have been.

Who Cheats?

For Tom and Tammy Taxpayer, tax cheating is just out
of the question. Tom, you know that Tammy gets the shakes

* CPA Institute Study, P. 12.

if you accidently run a stop sign; breaking the law is just
not the way of the Taxpayer Family or anybody you
know . . . . Or anybody you *think* you know! *In fact:*

• An IRS survey of 400 private-duty nurses—*nurses!*—
in New York City found *more than 90 percent* failing to report
all their income, and an average debt of $3,500 in back-
taxes.*

• An audit of 4,000 California returns containing large
deductions for *contributions to charity* (see Chapter 7) caught
the vast majority inflating their philanthropic impulses, and
owing an average of $5,000 in additional taxes. And one
recently reported state-of-the-art scam involves buying individual pieces of art or whole collections, having them appraised at a ridiculously high value and then donating them
to some unsuspecting museum for a wildly inflated
deduction.

• By one IRS estimate, about sixteen *thousand* individual "mail order ministries" have been created during
the past five years by those preaching a gospel of less taxes
through tax-immune private churches.

It can only mean that those willing to cheat on their
taxes by resorting to obfuscations in the name of charity,
art and religion, hold something else more sacred—the belief
that it's sometimes worth breaking Uncle Sam's laws if they
have to, in order not to pay up. And that belief may be becoming the norm.

In that 1980 survey commissioned by the IRS, 46 percent of those questioned agreed with the statement that
"People who openly refuse to pay taxes serve a useful purpose because they focus public attention on how the government spends money." Only half of those surveyed felt that
"People who try to persuade others to disobey the tax laws
are a threat to the country because they encourage revolt,"
and more than 43 percent of the younger surveyees agreed
that "People who disagree with how Federal tax money is

* "TAX CHEATING," *Time,* P. 26.

spent should have a right to refuse to pay some of their taxes."*

If younger people more than older ones are inclined to feel that tax protesting serves a useful purpose, so are blacks much more likely than whites to agree that "Stretching the truth a little in order to save $100 or less in taxes is not really tax cheating; it's more like exceeding the 55 mph speed limit because almost everyone does it."**

Study after study finds the young, the minorities, the typical working American, convinced that high-income earners and large business corporations are paying less than their fair share in taxes. The authors of the 1980 survey, for instance, note that "The perception that Congress is intentionally allowing wealthy taxpayers and big business to escape taxes legally can be a strong motivation for others to create their own tax savings,"*** and find "a growing perception that the IRS enforcement practices are applied in an uneven and inequitable fashion, whereby low-and middle-income taxpayers are harassed over small amounts, while insufficient attention is paid to the wealthy and especially to non-filers."****

In dollar terms alone, we've come a long way since that cold December day 210 years ago when a bunch of "tax protesters" soon-to-be American revolutionaries, sunk 342 tea chests to the bottom of Boston Harbor. A $120 billion "tax gap" ain't no tea party, especially for the large majority of Americans who continue dutifully to dole out the taxes they think they owe. Are we right to worry, as the CPA's do, that all the media attention focused on tax cheating may turn it into a self-fulfilling prophecy—that "it becomes easier to rationalize tax cheating on the grounds that 'everyone else is doing it' "?

Add it all up: what these otherwise basically honest hardworking Americans are reacting to, might just be the feel-

* CSR Survey, P. 63.
** CSR Survey, P. 67.
*** CSR Survey, P. 23.
**** CSR Survey, P. 23-24.

ing that tax shelters—a $12 billion industry by 1983—are created to abet lawful tax *avoidance* for the wealthy few, with out-and-out illegal tax *evasion* the only game in town left for the rest of them. And add to that, the perception that *how* this Administration *spends* its tax dollars is even less in their interest, and the makings of a true tax revolt by the self-assessed down-and-outs could really be in the making.

During the heyday of our Viet Nam involvement, a group of antiwar activists latched onto the idea of making their voice heard in Washington by withholding the excise taxes due on their monthly telephone bills. Before the movement ended, somewhere between eight to eleven thousand separate acts of excise-tax withholding had been logged by the IRS. But it ended nonetheless, before the War did, with the Taxman levying bank accounts and garnishing the wages of each and every one of the protesters he could get his ungloved hands on.

In 1982, by IRS calculations, 844 Americans filed "political protest" returns; that is, returns accompanied by underpayments of Federal income tax and an explicit politically-oriented explanation for the underpayment. The government is at pains to point out, correctly, how tiny that number is in comparison with the thousands who don't file or who underreport for more mundane reasons. But it's also worth noting that the number has almost *quintupled* since 1978. What's more, a growing branch of the nuclear-freeze movement is now starting to urge "tax resistance" as the clearest, loudest voice in opposition to ever-renewing rounds of senseless nuclear buildup.

The clearest, maybe—but not the cleanest. The Taxman regularly reminds Congress that for every additional dollar it will let him devote to enforcement activities, as many as twenty additional dollars of unlawfully evaded taxes can be collected. He will eagerly remind you that simply failing to file, supply information, keep proper records or pay taxes owed is a misdemeanor carrying fines up to $25,000 and or imprisonment up to a year, and that willfully attempting to

evade or defeat tax is a felony offering fines as high as
$100,000, up to five years in jail, or both. And he will point
out that the public is dead-wrong in its persistent belief that
jail is rarely, if ever, imposed for tax-cheating.

He is very unlikely, though to point out the alternative
every tax-paying American has to make her statement heard,
without risk of prosecution, by *using* the system instead of
abusing it to *avoid* paying income taxes *completely within
the bounds of the law.*

The evidence is there: a "tax revolt" seems undeniably
down the road. What still remains unsettled, however, is
what shape that revolt will take: Will it evolve into a massive
show of unlawful tax evasion, clogging the courts and divert-
ing the national attention from the real substance of the
revolt to the peripheral issue of respecting the tax laws
themselves? If so, half the battle's already lost, for there will
always be millions of progressive-minded Americans whose
basic belief in a just society just won't permit them to con-
done intentionally breaking the law.

On the other hand, the coming tax revolt could evolve
into something quite different: an army of low and middle-
income, progressive-minded working Americans taking up
the laws, and the tax breaks in those laws, as their most po-
tent weapon in the fight to bring a just society back. Tax
avoidance need not remain the refuge of the rich, as the rest
of this book has tried to point out. You don't have to be rich
not to pay taxes, Tom and Tammy, but you do have to take
a little time to study the tricks of the trade.

Conclusion

Tax reform? *Boring.*

Searching for a surefire way not to have to endure that loathsome round of office Christmas parties next year? Make sure you bring up reforming the tax system with every reveler you meet, and pretty soon word will get out to lock the door when you come by. After all, as one of our recent presidents said, sometimes life just isn't fair. It's bad enough all of us have to forage through a 1040 Form come every April; who in the world wants to spend any more time than absolutely necessary arguing about the technical merits of all this unpleasantness?

Maybe you do. Maybe proposals for a flat-rate tax, a gross income tax or a consumption tax bore you to distraction. Perhaps their intricacies and relative merits are best left to the experts. But here, just for fun, are a couple of facts about our *current* tax system you may want to ponder, puzzle over and put to your congressman the next time he asks you what's on your mind.

Fact: Our tax system respects those who make their money by *profits* much, much more than those who make their money by *working*. How so? By the explicit preference in the law for capital-gains income, versus ordinary income. If you earn a dollar in wages, it's taxed as "ordinary" income: at your full tax rate. If, on the other hand, you earn a dollar by selling some stock you've owned more than a year at a profit, that profit is taxed at "preferred" long-term capital gains rates, which are only 40 percent of your ordinary income tax rate.

Fact: Our tax system respects you if you're in business, more than if you're not. That used car you and Tammy bought this year to get to and from work in, you paid for with after-tax dollars, pure and simple; the tax system didn't play a role. But your next-door neighbor businessman drives his company car; when he bought it, he received an investment tax credit—a dollar-for-dollar reduction in taxes—for a good-

sized chunk of the purchase price. And until the day he sells
it, he'll be able to depreciate it, creating a continuing stream
of valuable deductions and still more tax savings.

Fact: Our tax system likes you better if you own
somebody else's home, than if you own your own. Not-
withstanding the special "shields" discussed in Chapter 4,
if you own your own home, you may not depreciate it—nor
may you take tax deductions for repairs, insurance, utilities
and so on. But if its's an investment "income property" you
own, the expense-related and depreciation-related deductions
it'll generate will go a very long way toward cancelling out
the taxes you owe. (Of course, if you can't afford your own
home and have to rent instead of paying a mortgage, sorry—
no tax benefits *at all.)*

Fact: The tax system likes you better if you're in the kind
of work that allows you to do business over lunch, than if
you're not. If you do business over lunch in a fancy restaurant
or nightclub, etc., a big part of the bill is a big tax deduction for someone at your table. If you eat your meal out of
a lunchbox with co-workers and discuss the weather, sorry—
Uncle Sam ain't interested in picking up part of the tab.

Fact: The tax system likes you better when you exercise
your Constitutional right to "petition the Government for
a redress of grievances"—to lobby, in other words—if your
cause is business-supportive, than if it's not business-
supportive. If Acme Missile Company spends millions call-
ing on Congress to deploy its product across Heartland
America, those lobbying expenses are considered a cost of
doing business and are tax-deductible to Acme. If you spend
two bucks on a long distance call to some junior legislative
aide trying to convince him otherwise, you just engaged in
a civic duty. Civic duties are not tax-deductible.

Fact: The tax system likes you better if you fly off to
fancy meetings with others in your own profession, than if
you go to night school to learn new skills. To a lawyer, doctor
or virtually every professional, the costs of conventions,
meetings and continuing-education courses are a well-

pursued tax-deductible business expense. But if you work all day and spend your spare time and sparse savings trying to educate your way into a better job, forget it—Uncle Sam doesn't want to know.

What's it all mean? It means, Tom and Tammy, that under the current tax system, as Rodney Dangerfield would say, you just don't get no respect. It means that our tax laws have been shaped, like so many of our other laws, to help especially those who were present at the shaping. You've taken the first step toward making our tax system work for you already, by starting to learn how to turn some of the existing tax-saving devices to your own advantage. Come April 16th, don't tuck this new awareness away in a drawer until same taxtime next year. Take the the *next* step, and take an interest in re-shaping this system of ours into one that treats *you* with respect.

Selected Grove Press Paperbacks

E863   ACKER, KATHY / Great Expectations: A Novel / $6.95

E835   BARASH, D. AND LIPTON, J. / Stop Nuclear War! A Handbook / $7.95

E96   BECKETT, SAMUEL / Endgame / $2.95

B78   BECKETT, SAMUEL / Three Novels: Molloy, Malone Dies, The Unnamable / $4.95

E33   BECKETT, SAMUEL / Waiting for Godot / $3.50

B108   BRECHT, BERTOLT / Mother Courage and Her Children / $2.45

B115   BURROUGHS, WILLIAM S. / Naked Lunch / $3.95

E773   CLURMAN, HAROLD (Ed.) / Nine Plays of the Modern Theater (Waiting For Godot by Samuel Beckett, The Visit by Friedrich Dürrenmatt, Tango by Slawomir Mrozek, The Caucasian Chalk Circle by Bertolt Brecht, The Balcony by Jean Genet, Rhinoceros by Eugene Ionesco, American Buffalo by David Mamet, The Birthday Party by Harold Pinter, Rosencrantz and Guildenstern are Dead by Tom Stoppard) / $11.95

B342   FANON, FRANTZ / The Wretched of the Earth / $4.95

E792   GETTLEMAN, MARVIN, et. al., eds. / El Salvador: Central America in the New Cold War / $8.95

E881   HITLER, ADOLF / Hitler's Secret Book / $7.95

E101   IONESCO, EUGENE / Four Plays (The Bald Soprano, The Lesson, The Chairs, and Jack, or The Submission) / $4.95

E259   IONESCO, EUGENE / Rhinoceros and Other Plays / $4.95

E697   MAMET, DAVID / American Buffalo / $3.95

B10   MILLER, HENRY / Tropic of Cancer / $3.95

B59   MILLER, HENRY / Tropic of Capricorn / $3.95

E411   PINTER, HAROLD / The Homecoming / $4.95

E744   POMERANCE, BERNARD / The Elephant Man / $4.25

B438   REAGE, PAULINE / Story of O, Part II: Return to the Chateau / $3.95

B313   SELBY, HUBERT / Last Exit to Brooklyn / $2.95

E763   SHAWN, WALLACE and GREGORY, ANDRE / My Dinner with Andre / $5.95

E618   SNOW, EDGAR / Red Star Over China / $8.95

B319   STOPPARD, TOM / Rosencrantz and Guildenstern Are Dead / $2.95

B341   SUZUKI, D. T. / An Introduction to Zen Buddhism / $2.95

B474   TOOLE, JOHN KENNEDY / A Confederacy of Dunces / $3.95

GROVE PRESS, INC., 196 West Houston St., New York, N.Y. 10014